GOD SEEKER

BY THIS AUTHOR

God-Seeker

———

These Hands That Hold the World

FICTION TITLES

Goleah's Lore

———

Age of the Anathema series

Tainted

Branded

SHORT STORIES
The Dead Were Never from Florida
Morpheus: Tales of the Karsha

GOD SEEKER

The Complete Collection

XYVAH OKOYE

GOD SEEKER
THE COMPLETE COLLECTION
This omnibus edition published by Chartus.X. 2022

Thy will be done copyright ©Xyvah Okoye, 2014
Understanding Christianity copyright ©Xyvah Okoye, 2016
Chasing God copyright ©Xyvah Okoye, 2020
Show me Your Glory copyright ©Xyvah Okoye, 2021
Why Christians go to Church copyright ©Xyvah Okoye, 2022

The production of this book was sponsored by Dr. Tonye Wokoma.
Editorial Team: The Derah, Neliya Dalu, Priye Okoye

All rights reserved under international copyright law. This book is copyright under the Berne Convention. No reproduction without written permission from the publisher.
The moral right of Xyvah Okoye to be identified as the author of this work has been asserted in accordance with the Copyright, Designs and Patents Act of 1988.

Hardback ISBN: 978-1-915129-02-4, Paperback ISBN: 978-1-915129-06-2, eBook ISBN: 978-1-915129-07-9, Audiobook ISBN: 978-1-915129-18-5

Excerpts from Kohlenberger, J.R., Swanson, J.A. (2001). The Strongest Strong's Exhaustive Concordance of the Bible. Michigan: Zondervan.

Unless otherwise stated, all scripture quotations are taken from the King James Version of the Bible.

For anyone seeking intimacy with God

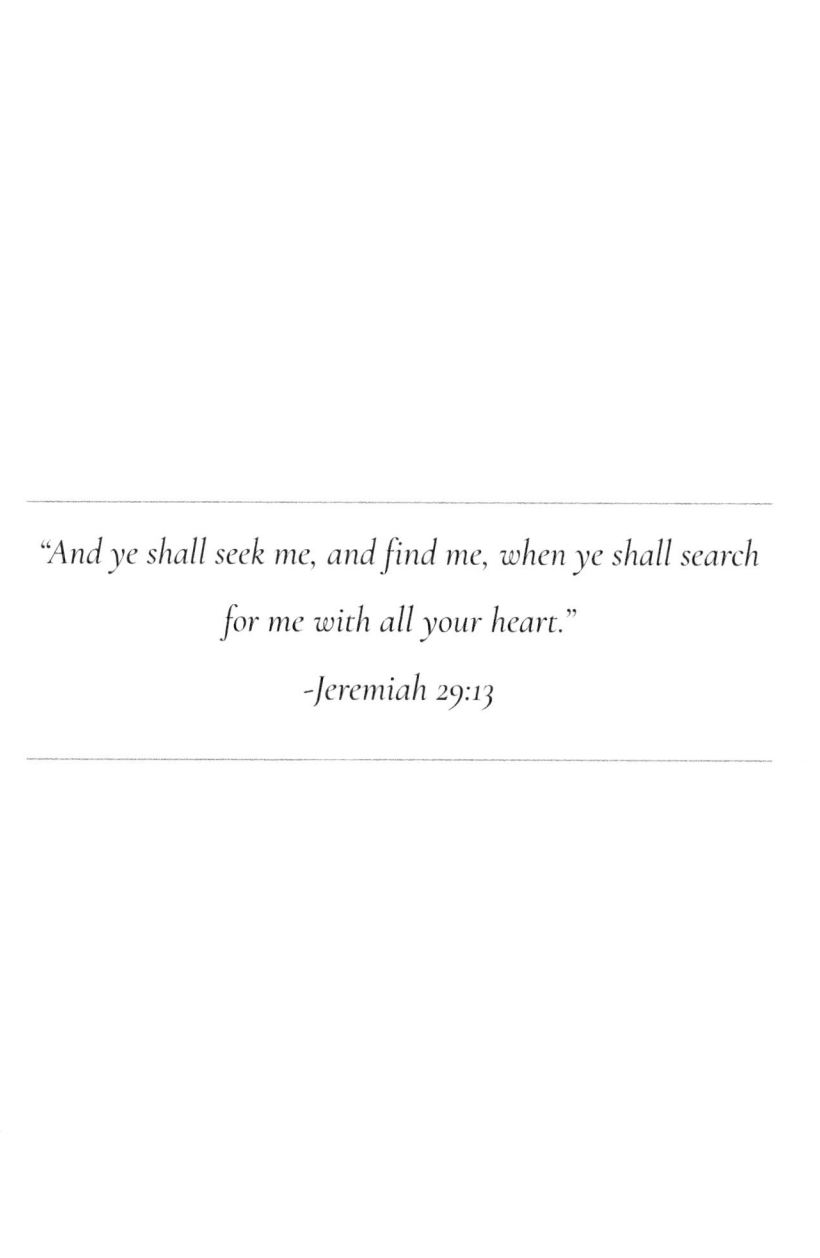

"And ye shall seek me, and find me, when ye shall search for me with all your heart."

-Jeremiah 29:13

TABLE OF CONTENT

INTRODUCTION
UNDERSTANDING CHRISTIANITY

1. What Is Christianity? 1
2. The Process Of Christianity 3
3. The Concept Of Gospel Salvation 7
4. To The Saving Of The Soul 18
5. The Cornerstone of Christianity 21
6. That I May Know Him 25

THY WILL BE DONE

7. The Right Thing 33
8. How To Know What God Thinks Is Right 35
9. Doing The Right Thing 39
10. Justification By Faith 41
11. The Faith Of Abel 42
12. The Way 48
13. Growing In God 51
14. Seasons 53
15. Different Seasons Of Life 55
16. Four (4) Stages Of Life And Ministry 58
17. Rewards Of Righteousness 68
18. The Path Of Righteousness 70

19. For His Name's Sake 77

CHASING GOD

20. Beginning With Salvation 81
21. From A Background Of Nothingness 85
22. Leaving And Cleaving 91
23. Covenant Relationships 94
24. Putting Others First 97
25. Laying A Good Foundation 103
26. Dealing With The Past 107
27. The Key To Relationships 111
28. What It Means To Be A Friend Of Jesus 119
29. Faith And Belief 124
30. Faith And The Knowledge Of God 127
31. Faith And Hearing 134
32. Faith And Obedience 138
33. Faith And Speaking 145
34. While We Wait 148

SHOW ME YOUR GLORY

35. The Hand Of David 159
36. Eight Characteristics Of David 165
37. The Meaning Of The Presence 176
38. Signs Of The Presence Of God 182

39. The Anointing..186

40. Forty Days In His Presence.................................190

41. The Purpose Of The Presence.............................192

42. Called To Witness..210

43. The Ministry 215

44. Building The Wall..224

WHY CHRISTIANS GO TO CHURCH

Part 1: The Church

45. Basic Christianity 237

46. Understanding The Church................................238

47. 7 Reasons Why The Church Is Important 244

48. 10 Things That Happen In The Church............248

49. Church Membership 256

50. 3 Rewards Of Being A Stable Church Member........259

51. Different Churches, Different Doctrines 262

52. Church Leadership 271

53. How To Relate With Church Leadership.................276

54. 7 Reasons Why Every Christian Should Go To Church278

Part 2: Reasons Christians Give For Not Going To Church

55. Church Is Boring...283

56. Christians Don't Get Along 286

57. I Feel I Don't Belong...288

58. People In Church Are Proud 290

59. People In Church Are Nosy Snitches Who Report Everything To The Pastor 292
60. There Are So Many Things Wrong With The Church 295
61. People Idolise Preachers 298
62. Christians Are Hypocrites 301
63. God Is Everywhere And Jesus Is In My Heart 303
64. Other Excuses 305
65. More Types Of People You Will Find In The Church 310
66. A Word Of Caution 316
67. Bibliography iii

GOD SEEKER

The Complete Collection

INTRODUCTION

This book is a collection of teachings, written to guide all those who are seeking God. It is made up of 5 parts which touch on different aspects of the journey, beginning with Understanding the concept of Christianity itself.

Part 1, Understanding Christianity, deals with the very basics of the religion and relationship with God.

Part 2, Thy Will be done, focusses on building the believer's relationship with God, flowing into deeper truths and more complex realities as we get to part 3, Chasing God.

This third section takes a closer look at various aspects of the journey to knowing God more intimately. Oftentimes, in this section, when referring to those in authority, the word father is used. Please be aware that this is gender neutral and does not necessarily mean one's natural or birth parent.

In part 4, Show me Your Glory, the emphasis is on the manifest presence of God, birthed in intimacy and brought forth with a purpose. The first part of this section refers to being a musician because I am one. However, these truths and principles are applicable to all aspects of one's life and calling.

The final part, Why Christians go to Church, deals with understanding the Church of God and how it fits with the life of the believer.

Each part of this book can be read independently, though one will get a sense of progression in their understanding and experience of the journey to finding and knowing God by reading it as compiled.

This book is a guide. There is still so much to learn and experience in finding intimacy with God, but my prayer is that this will be a great starting point and will assist in the journey to a deep relationship with God.

UNDERSTANDING CHRISTIANITY

WHAT IS CHRISTIANITY?

"Then Barnabas went on to Tarsus to look for Saul. When he found him, he brought him back to Antioch. Both of them stayed there with the church for a full year, teaching large crowds of people. (It was at Antioch that the believers were first called Christians.)"
-Acts 11:25-26 (New Living Translation)

The earth has existed for thousands of years, and many have walked upon it, leaving footprints etched in both sand and stone to guide us through this wilderness we call life. One of the many paths we tread towards understanding and enlightenment is that which we call religion.

Religion, in its most basic sense, is a system of faith in and worship of a supernatural being or power that controls (or at least affects) one's life. It is a controversial and complicated subject, and this is the reason I have taken the time to explain Christianity in such a way that uncomplicates things.

A plethora of people who call themselves Christians have no idea what it truly means to be one.

The name "Christian" was given by the people of Antioch to the believers who came after Christ. This name was given to them because they were like The Christ, the Anointed One, the Messiah. This Anointed One refers to Jesus.

The resemblance between the disciples and Jesus was clear enough for the people of Antioch to describe them as being Christ-like.

In the most basic of terms, this is what it really means to be a Christian. It is to be someone so transformed by the teachings of Christ that it is obvious you follow him even without you declaring it.

THE PROCESS OF CHRISTIANITY

"For whom he did foreknow, he also did predestinate to be conformed to the image of his Son, that he might be the firstborn among many brethren."

-Romans 8:29

Many believe the change which happens in becoming a Christian takes place overnight. They do not understand that Christianity is a process. Often, believers backslide or do not really get the full benefit of Christianity because they do not understand what exactly has happened to them in Christ.

Christianity is not a new set of rules or even a new way of life. It is a process of faith-inspired growth which takes place due to an intimate personal relationship with Jesus Christ. As Dag Heward-Mills so perfectly puts it in his book, *Gospel Salvation*, "Christ will change your heart and give you power to control your body and renew your mind."

This process we call Christianity can take any length of time, depending on the individual and their level of intimacy with Christ. Christian or spiritual growth is not really determined by how much you do, but by how much your character is changed to conform to that of Christ.

The reason we don't just die and go to heaven once we receive and accept Christ, is because God still has work for us to do, both by and within us. One's character needs to be changed and shaped in holiness. The believer must be purged of the sin and iniquity that is ingrained in their personality, and be presented to God, holy and without blemish, sanctified and cleansed. Without this, one cannot get to heaven. (See Galatians 5:19-21.)

Being born again does not guarantee entry to heaven. Heaven is God's home, and only His children will be allowed entry. This is why He sent Christ to come to be the first-born of many brethren.

By dying on the cross, Christ gave believers the power to become children of God and opened the way to be with God. Being born again gives the believer the ability or power to become a child of God; it doesn't automatically make them one. (See John 1:12.)

In John 3, Jesus explained this to Nicodemus, a Pharisee who came to him one night.

The Pharisees were a Jewish sect, the religious leaders of that day. They were the stewards of the power and presence of God. They were supposedly His spokespeople and chosen vessels. Nicodemus came to Jesus because Jesus had the power, authority and miracles the Pharisees were supposed to have. Jesus walked in the ministry that

Nicodemus and his sect were supposed to be walking in.

Old Nick probably wondered how Jesus had the power and authority to manifest such a ministry. Nicodemus wanted to know the secret to having God with him, so he snuck out one night to ask Jesus. The Pharisee said to Jesus (I paraphrase), "I know you have God. I know you're walking in the power and in the kingdom and in the authority of God."

Nicodemus asked Christ for a secret. He wanted to know how to have the kingdom of God manifested in his life as well; he wanted to have the presence of God in his life. Jesus explained to him that these things would not happen in his life and ministry until he was born again.

Jesus teaches here that no one can see the manifested kingdom, rule, or authority of God if they are not born again. The power of God is a privilege reserved for those who are born again.

However, being born again, as Jesus explained to Old Nick later, is only the first step. In being born again, a believer receives power to *become* a child of God, to see the Kingdom of God on earth, but not the power to *inherit* it.

Old Nick marvelled. Who wouldn't? Jesus was telling him that he needed to be born again. Did this mean he had to return to his mother's womb and be reborn to enter heaven? Or was Jesus referring to being reincarnated into the same family (which was likely impossible because his mother was probably dead or too old to have children anyway)?

Jesus explained to Nicodemus that that was not the case. He explained that what Nick was looking for came by being born of water and of the Spirit. Becoming a child of God would happen by being born of the Spirit and of water.

Like most trying to decipher Jesus's cryptic words, Nicodemus must have been confused out of his mind. Kindly, Jesus took the time to explain what he means in John 3:4-7. Being born again is a simple way of saying a person has been born of the Spirit. It means the person exists as a result of the Spirit. The person's existence is as a result of (and therefore governed by) the Spirit of God.

Becoming a child of God who would enter the kingdom of heaven is a process that begins with true and total surrender to the Spirit of God. This is the rebirth commonly referred to as *receiving salvation* or *being born again*. Once this process is begun, the believer is gradually changed and moulded until they are conformed to the image of Christ.

THE CONCEPT OF GOSPEL SALVATION

"For I am not ashamed of the gospel of Christ: for it is the power of God unto salvation to every one that believeth; to the Jew first, and also to the Greek."

-Romans 1:16

In the previous chapter, we looked at what being born again means. Here, we learn a bit more about how it actually happens.

The Bible says the gospel of Jesus Christ is the power of God that leads to (or brings about) salvation to all who believe. The gospel of Jesus Christ is what brings about the rebirth of the believer. Without it, one cannot be born of the Spirit, and in turn, cannot become a child of God.

The word "salvation" is translated from the Greek noun "*Sōtēria*," meaning "rescue," or "deliverance." Through the gospel, believers are given power that will deliver them from danger, power that brings about a rebirth. This delivering power enables the believer to be conformed to the image of Christ—to be born again.

With this simple analysis, it is safe to conclude that the gospel of

Jesus Christ is the power that delivers believers from danger by changing them to become more like Christ. This knowledge is unfruitful without a true understanding of, a). What the gospel of Jesus Christ is, and b). What danger it is delivering the believer from.

THE GOSPEL OF JESUS CHRIST

The former treatise have I made, O Theophilus, of all that Jesus began both to do and teach, Until the day in which he was taken up, after that he through the Holy Ghost had given commandments unto the apostles whom he had chosen:

-Acts 1:1-2

The word "gospel" means "good news." The gospel of Jesus Christ is therefore the good news of Jesus Christ. This good news is explained by the author of the book of Acts, Dr. Luke, to be divided into two categories: the things Jesus did, and the things Jesus taught.

WHAT JESUS DID

What Jesus came to accomplish by his life, death and resurrection is easily gleaned from the acts he carried out while on earth. The words, teachings and acts of Jesus are topics that have received extensive study over the years because, as mentioned, these things make up the gospel of Jesus Christ which is the power the believer needs in order to become a child of God.

However, it would be beneficial to go a bit further back in order to understand why Jesus had to come to earth in the first place.

In Colossians 1:16, and John 1:3, we are told that all things were created by Jesus, for his good pleasure.

In the beginning, God (through and for Jesus) created the heavens and earth. He then formed the earth, setting boundaries, sprouting vegetation, and creating animals, all to bring forth after their own kind. God loved all of creation so much that He thought carefully about who would take care of it for Him. All the animals and the plants were created as an expression of Himself. They were created to show His Glory, not to take care of one another.

Since God was the only one actually capable of caring for the world as it was designed to be, He decided to create someone especially just to look after it. He created this person to be like Him, to love the world the way He did and to care for it the way He would. He called this person "Man." (See Genesis 1.)

After God made man (whom we shall call Man, because he was not named at this point), He did not throw him right in the deep end and say, "Here's the whole world, take care of it!" No, He curtained off a portion of the world, gathered a bit of everything Man would have to deal with in the world, and placed Man there to *learn* to tend it.

Sidenote: Even natural, God-given talents must be trained and honed to produce the optimum results.

So, Man is placed in this virtual-training-garden that God has created—Eden—and he must now learn to look after God's creations. To help him to work effectively, God pays him regular visits, giving him tutorials on how to handle things. God talks to him, fellowships with him, and finds out if there are any challenges he is facing.

Then one day, as God is observing Man's progress, He realises Man is lonely and in need of help. God seeks to give him a helper but cannot find anyone who actually meets Man's needs. So, God decides to create one. He puts Man to sleep, takes one of his ribs, and forms a helper out of it. When Man wakes, he calls this helper "Woman." (See Genesis 2.)

God leaves Man in the garden and Woman with him to help, visiting them regularly and fellowshipping with them. Till one day, the Serpent (whom we shall call Serps) comes to present Woman with a proposal to eat from a tree God instructed Man not to eat from. Mind you, this was the only tree Man was not allowed to eat from, and the reason God had given was that the day Man ate from it, he would die.

Serps told Woman that God never said they would die for eating the forbidden fruit, but rather, the fruit would give them the knowledge that would make them like God. Now, this was a tempting offer because Man and Woman were both in Eden to learn how to care for all of creation how God wanted. They were created like God (in His image and likeness) and were learning to be like God, so eating a fruit which sped up that process could not be bad, right?

Wrong.

Woman reached for the fruit, hand trembling as she anticipated the inevitable. When her palm closed about it and nothing happened, she held her breath and plucked the fruit.

For moments afterwards, she and Serps waited with bated breath. But, again, nothing happened.

"I told you nothing would happen," Serps mused. "Think about it: why would God put the answer to all your problems right in front of you, and then tell you not to eat it? I'm sure Man misunderstood the instruction."

Nodding solemnly, Woman stared at the fruit in her hand, considering the facts. It was true God wanted them to be like Him, so why would He deny them the one thing that would help them fulfil that purpose? Surely, Man had to be wrong about that.

"Well, what are you waiting for?" Serps slithered about the tree trunk, eyeing the fruit with malicious glee.

"I don't know," Woman confessed, "I mean, Man doesn't mix things up that badly. What if I'm wrong? I mean, what if you're wrong and this fruit is horrible and poisonous and..." She stared at the fruit. It didn't look poisonous. Or horrible. And if Serps was right and it did in fact make her like God, then she would be a fool not to try it.

"Taste it," Serps whispered, "see for yourself that I am not wrong."

Carefully, Woman raised the fruit to her mouth. She shut her eyes, breathed in deep, and took a tentative bite.

Silence. Nothing but silence.

Then the world came back into focus, clearer and brighter and better than she had known before. Because before, she had not known. Or seen. Or understood.

"I told you," Serps hissed, uncoiling himself from the tree. "You're not dead, and now you know Man was mistaken."

Woman smiled. She was alive. And she knew—*truly knew*—what she had to do next.

With knowledge on her side, it did not take much for Woman to tempt Man to share in her folly. She had eaten the fruit God had instructed them not to. No matter the reason God had given for His instruction, she had disobeyed Him. They both had. And they both knew it was wrong.

By this act of disobedience, Man and Woman had gained knowledge. But this knowledge had come by breaking God's trust, and that cost them dearly.

The ensuing fallout between Man, Woman and God brought about a separation between them. It brought a curse upon the land, upon the animals, and on Man and Woman, and even Serps.

In disobeying God, humanity was separated from him, leaving them at the mercy of the one who had sought to bring about this divide, the same one who had rebelled against God aeons before, taking with him a third of the host of heaven. By this one act, humanity, and all God had given them was surrendered to the devil.

But God loved humanity, and all His creation. So, He began planning a way to get His beloved humanity back. The plan He came up with to reconcile creation back to Him: Salvation through Jesus Christ.

This was a multi-step process. The first step was delivering humanity from the clutches of the devil. A price had to be paid for Man's and Woman's wrongdoing to, in a sense, buy humanity's freedom from the devil. And like any businessman worth his salt, the devil's asking price was not cheap. Well, what would you expect when demand is high and only you can fulfil it?

The second step was dealing with sin, that initial transgression that breached God's trust and damned all of humanity. After all, there was no point paying for their freedom if they were only going to reject God and break His trust again.

So, plans were made, and off Jesus went, down to the earth to save humanity. He knew and accepted the price the devil had demanded for humanity's freedom: blood. The devil knew Jesus was on a mission to save creation, but clearly he did not know how Jesus planned to accomplish it. I suppose, at this point, you're probably wondering the same thing.

The devil's final offer was for blood to be shed. He would accept nothing less for humanity's freedom. This meant God could only have His humans after they died—which was counterintuitive, because if they were not reconciled to Him before they died, then they could not come to be with Him after they did. This meant eternal separation from God who is all things good, leaving humanity in eternal suffering.

By dying as the lowest of sinners, Jesus, the Son of God, sacrificed himself in humanity's place. This freed humanity from being the devil's property, and opened up the avenue for reconciliation with God. This avenue is still open to all willing to believe in the price Jesus paid for them. This was what Jesus did.

Before his death, Jesus spent his life teaching about and demonstrating the power and principles of the kingdom of God. He spent his days showing and telling humanity how to reconcile with God, how to have a personal relationship with God and how to live like His child. These teachings are the cornerstone of salvation. These teachings are the lifeblood of Christianity, they are the power that transforms the heart of a believer. Believing in and acting on these teachings are the true essence of being born again.

And the very God of peace sanctifies you wholly; and I pray God your whole spirit and soul and body be preserved blameless unto the coming of our Lord Jesus Christ.

-1 Thessalonians 5:23

If Jesus, by dying for us, has saved us from hell and made us a new creation, then why does he say that he has given us the power to be saved? Why does the Bible then say that he has given us the power to become sons of God?

This is because man is a spirit, has a soul and lives in a body. We learn this from the apostle Paul in the above verse.

Human beings, you and I, are actually spirits which possess souls and dwell temporarily in our physical bodies. Jesus died to free our spirits, but our souls still need to choose God because it is our souls that need to be reformed and cleansed and remade into people God can trust as friends and family.

This segues nicely into what Jesus taught while he was on earth.

WHAT JESUS TAUGHT

And his disciples asked him, saying, What might this parable be? And he said, Unto you it is given to know the mysteries of the kingdom of God: but to others in parables; that seeing they might not see, and hearing they might not understand.

-Luke 8:9-10

Jesus taught a lot about the Kingdom of God. He did a lot of this teaching through parables for more reasons than the fact that everyone loves a great story. When Jesus's disciples asked him why he taught in parables to the people but spoke to them plainly, he told them it was because it wasn't for the people to understand.

The teachings of the kingdom were a club secret. Not everyone could know about it, because not everyone believed, so not everyone would understand. The simple requirement for understanding the teachings (which include the ways and keys) of the Kingdom is to become a part of this kingdom by being born again—believing in and accepting the price Jesus paid for your freedom, hereby choosing to reconcile with God.

As you may have noticed, the definition of being born again seems to grow or morph slightly each time. This is because, with more knowledge and understanding, layers are being stripped away to reveal deeper truths about our journey to being with God. It begins with being born of the Spirit, which in itself begins with accepting that Jesus paid the price for us to reconcile with God, and then going on to actually reconcile with Him by becoming how He created us to be—in His image and likeness.

This *becoming* part is where the teachings of Christ come in.

When one believes and accepts Jesus as the one who died to set them free, God sends His Spirit to be with them, to guide, teach, and help them on their journey back to Him. This Holy Spirit, the precious Gift of God, is the key to unlocking the parables Jesus taught. The Holy Spirit is the one who will teach the believer the truths about the Kingdom of God, and help them live out those truths, thus conforming them to Christ's image. (See John 16:7-16.)

TO THE SAVING OF THE SOUL

"Wherefore lay apart all filthiness and superfluity of naughtiness, and receive with meekness the engrafted word, which is able to save your souls."

-James 1:21

When we die, we take nothing with us. We leave everything behind, including our bodies. The only thing that remains with the spirit when we die is the soul.

The soul is made up of one's character and attitude, one's intellect and emotions. If the soul is full of sin, one can't enter heaven. The soul can be described as being made up of many layers which become difficult to change the older one gets. These layers include our attitudes, emotions, intellect, thoughts, and innate character.

These aspects of the soul have been created by factors such as upbringing, genetics, experiences, circumstances, and so on. They have produced the unique personality that each individual possesses. If the soul is not purged of sin (that same willingness to break God's trust in pursuit of our own passions), the person who possesses it cannot inherit the Kingdom of God. (See 1 Corinthians 6:9-10.)

God is a Spirit, and He has saved and rejuvenated our spirits because we have been bought by the blood of Jesus. However, He will not save our souls because they belong to us. Remember, man is a spirit, has a soul and lives in a body.

Each person is responsible for the soul they possess. They are responsible for the changing and reformation of their soul. This is why, in accepting Jesus's sacrifice, the believer receives (from God) the power to save their own soul. (See Romans 12:2.)

The Bible says God is just. He is fair, He works based on principles. God has given each person a will. God gave the first Man and Woman their own will, He gave them the ability to choose between Him and anything else. When God made the Garden of Eden, He placed both the trees of life and the knowledge of good and evil in the garden, giving Man a choice. There is no free will to choose if there are no options to choose from. He gave Man the option to trust and obey Him or not.

God does not impose His will on anyone, and He will not take away all the sin and evil in this world either. There will come a time when He purges the earth of sin and wickedness, but that time is not now. Now, God allows both the good and the evil to flourish together because He wants people who will honestly love and worship Him from their hearts, and there is no greater way to prove the purity of one's love than by choosing Him of one's own free will.

(See John 4:23-24, Ephesians 5:26-27.)

Daily, the choice is placed before every believer as they run the Christian race: Will one choose to depend on their knowledge of right and wrong, what they have decided is the best option? Or will they choose to surrender their life and will to God by obeying His Word?

When one chooses to follow and depend on their own knowledge of good and evil, they plunge their life into further darkness, chaos and ruin, but when one depends on the Lord, trusting that He knows what is best, their soul is changed and transformed, purged and purified.

When one chooses to follow Christ and surrenders their will to him by obeying his word, that is the point at which the salvation of the soul begins. And this process, step by step, day by day, decision after decision, is what is known as *Christianity*.

THE CORNERSTONE OF CHRISTIANITY

"Now therefore ye are no more strangers and foreigners, but fellowcitizens with the saints, and of the household of God; And are built upon the foundation of the apostles and prophets, Jesus Christ himself being the chief corner stone;"

-Ephesians 2:19-20

In the 8th chapter of his letter to the believers in Rome, apostle Paul explained the process of Christianity. He explained that those who believe in the sacrifice of Jesus are on a different path from those that do not. By their faith, the believer has been delivered from condemnation and set on a path to renewing their mind.

To walk this straight and narrow path, the believer has been given the gift of the Holy Spirit as a helper. The Holy Spirit, who knows the heart and mind of God, will guide the believer to becoming more like Christ with each choice they make.

Paul explains that this is one major difference between the believers and those that do not believe in Jesus. The unbeliever's decisions are guided by their flesh (senses and desires) which can be influenced by many outside sources, both physical and spiritual. The Word of God and the Holy Spirit guide the believer's decisions.

However, if the believer chooses not to walk according to the guidance of the Holy Spirit, they will still be condemned on the last day because the salvation Christ began in their spirit is not complete until their soul has also been changed.

The apostle goes on to explain that God has predestined believers, from before the foundations of the earth, to be His sons and daughters. God sent Christ to earth to be an example to the believer of what His child ought to be like. Paul explains that it is the children of God who inherit the kingdom with Christ. Seeing as Christ is the example of what a child of God should be like, unless one becomes like Christ, one has no chance of getting to heaven.

Jesus was sent to be an example, to lead and guide believers down the path of salvation. Jesus is the greatest example a believer could ever have. He is the mark, the standard of Christianity.

True spiritual growth is measured by how Christ-like one is. It is based on one's character and nature being like that of Christ. Everyone alive today who calls themselves a Christian is still in the process of becoming like Christ.

One may not appear to be as sinful as some other person, or one's faults may not be so glaringly obvious, but one still has faults in their soul that need to be worked on. That is why the Bible teaches not to judge, criticise or condemn one another, or to look down on others. Thinking one is better than others, in itself, is a huge character flaw that needs to be fixed.

Jesus teaches love above all else: To love God and love one another, not because people are perfect but because God loves each individual and is patiently helping them, working in and with them to correct their faults and purge them from all their sins and iniquity.

So, when God is working patiently and tirelessly to help someone deal with a character flaw and one stands by, criticising them about it, what one is unwittingly doing is teaming up with the devil, the accuser of the brethren, to tear that person down. As soon as one does that, they pitch themselves against God.

It is necessary to be very careful how one treats and interacts with others, especially those of the household of faith, because Christ shed his blood for them and lives right now making intercession for believers before God.

If Christ, who suffered and died for the sinner is interceding for that person, then why are those who have neither suffered nor died standing in judgement of them? If Christ, who went through death to deal with sin, has not yet condemned them, then why should anyone else?

As Christians, Christ is the standard. Christianity is the process of being conformed to his image, but most believers could not recognise Christ if he stood right in front of them. Knowing the image one is to be conformed to plays a huge part in the changing process. This is why believers must not only talk about and read about Christ, but know him on a personal level.

Intimacy with Christ is built on the foundation of daily interaction with the Word of God, in which the Holy Spirit reveals the person of Christ to the believer.

THAT I MAY KNOW HIM

"That I may know him, and the power of his resurrection, and the fellowship of his sufferings, being made conformable unto his death;"

- Philippians 3:10

When Jesus walked the earth, he called 12 disciples to be with him. To these twelve disciples, he revealed himself and The Father. He taught them about the Kingdom of God, showing them secrets that no man knew.

These twelve disciples came to know him intimately and went on to preach the gospel in power and in his spirit, also being conformed to his image.

The apostle John describes this experience and explains to the people that he talks about his experience with Christ because he wants them to have it too. (See 1 John 1:1-4.)

The Apostle Paul was called to the service of God by Jesus himself when Paul was on the road to Damascus, on a mission to persecute the believers of the early church. Jesus appeared to him and instructed him on what to do. Paul surrendered his life to The Lord that day, blind for three days while he prayed to God.

He received his healing and was led to join the Church, where he remained for at least three years with the apostles Peter and John, learning from them all that he could about Jesus. Then he left to preach the gospel and fulfil the call of God upon his life.

Throughout his life, Paul strove with zeal and a persistent effort, building the Church, preaching the gospel, teaching and encouraging believers, for one main reason: To know Jesus and be conformed to his image. (See Philippians 3:7-14.)

Paul is a great example of someone in the same situation as the modern Christian. Paul, unlike the other apostles, did not know Jesus while he was on earth. Paul did not get the chance to walk with Jesus, to eat with him, travel with him and be taught of him like the other disciples did. He was called by Christ and sent to a man who then led him to other men who told him about Jesus.

This is the same situation most modern-day Christians find themselves in. They heard Christ calling them, tugging at their heart, they responded and were instructed to go to a person who taught them or (probably) led them to other people who taught them about Christ.

The difference between Paul's situation and that of the modern-day believer's is that Paul did more, achieved more, and went further than most Christians go these days. And that is because his aim and motivation, his one vision and greatest desire in life, was to know Christ and to become like him. He fixed his eyes on Jesus, looking unto him as the beginning and the end of it all, the author and finisher of his faith.

Paul strove more than anything to know Jesus personally. He learnt from the disciples all he could about Jesus and what Jesus said about knowing him, then he went on to tell the churches about Jesus and how to know him for themselves.

When we study Peter's first sermon in the book of Acts, chapter two, and the recorded sermons of the other apostles, we see that preaching the Gospel of Jesus Christ consists of the two things we learned: Preaching what Jesus did to save humanity, and teaching on how to know him personally.

Knowing God personally is the something I am passionate about. I believe everyone will benefit greatly from an intimate relationship with Jesus Christ, whether one wants to bear it under the banner of religion, faith, tradition, culture, or even relationship. Knowing Jesus is key.

★★★

If one would like to begin their relationship with Jesus today, they may start by saying this prayer, believing that Jesus Christ is the son of God who died to save them;

Dear Lord,

Thank you for your sacrifice to buy me my freedom from sin. Please wash away my sins with the blood of Jesus.

Today I accept the Holy Spirit—my counsellor and comforter, my gift from you—into my heart, that I may know you, in both suffering and glory.

Thank you, Jesus, for loving me, for dying for me, for what you have done for me, and for all you will continue to do for me.

Thank you, Lord, for saving me.

Amen.

It is true that the cares of life and the deceitfulness of riches can turn one's focus away from seeking Christ. Therefore, I will not neglect the truth that some who have dedicated their lives to Christ do sometimes grow distant from God. In these cases, they only need to acknowledge they have sinned, and turn back to God in repentance. Saying the above prayer sincerely is a simple way to reconnect with Christ.

Remember, Christianity is a process, and building intimacy with Christ is a daily experience. After saying this prayer in faith, it is crucial to find a Holy Bible—and a church with sound biblical teachings—to learn more about Christ and the ways of the Kingdom as they walk this journey to knowing, loving, and being like Christ.

More information on growing in intimacy with Christ can be found in my book, *Chasing God*. To learn more about the Church and its role in the life of the believer, my book, *Why Christians go to Church,* provides answers.

THY WILL BE DONE

THE RIGHT THING

"But seek ye first the kingdom of God, and his righteousness; and all these things shall be added unto you."

-Matthew 6:33

Varying opinions of right and wrong exist, revealing to us that the word "right" cannot be defined objectively. Right and wrong are subject to communal as well as individual standards and beliefs.

The word translated in the above scripture to mean *Righteousness* is derived from the Greek word, *"Dikaiosune,"* which means *"Right-doing."* Simply put, *righteousness* refers to doing the right thing.

Right-doing speaks of completeness, correctness, the most appropriate thing in a given situation. It is what is considered normal, factual, or sound in any given place or time, and it is subject to varying standards.

In this book, we will look at doing the right thing according to God's standards, learning how to determine what is considered right by God, and understanding how to live in the Righteousness of God.

To do this, we first should understand the importance of Righteousness.

Without rules, a community cannot thrive. The regulations which dictate the norms of a society help keep order in that society. For peace to exist among people with different individual experiences, beliefs and levels of understanding, boundaries must be set. Acceptable ways of behaviour must be expressly stated and agreed upon.

Rules and regulations must be put in place.

These rules and regulations set up by each society determine what is right and what is wrong according to the tenets of that society.

In the society of Christians or God-Chasers—a society regulated by God and His Church—right and wrong are determined by God.

HOW TO KNOW WHAT GOD THINKS IS RIGHT

"For as he thinketh in his heart, so is he..."

-Proverbs 23:7

Our actions are a direct result of our thoughts. Our perceptions and understanding of the world around us cause us to view situations in certain ways.

For example, someone who has an innate belief that spiders are deadly would think of every spider they see as a potential threat to their existence and would behave in a manner that they think befits the situation.

Some people search them out to kill them while others avoid them altogether. Whereas someone who absolutely loves spiders and thinks they are fascinating creatures would search them out to breed and study them.

These are very different behaviours, caused by different thought processes.

Our behaviours are moulded upon the skeleton of our thought processes. In other words, the way we behave depends on the way we think. God does not think the way we do, and that's why He does not behave the way we do.

Seeing there is a vast difference between the ways we and God think, we are bound to be living by very different standards of righteousness. This is why Christ instructed us to *seek* God's own standard of righteousness. (See Matthew 6.)

Because we do not think like God, and therefore do not know what God thinks, one will do well to wonder, "How does one then attain to God's standards of right-living? How can one possibly know what God thinks is right?"

The answer is simple: *ask*.

Jesus reveals this when he teaches his disciples how to pray in Matthew 6. He teaches them to seek *first* the kingdom of God *and* His righteousness. He tells them that after the greetings and catching up when coming to the Heavenly Father, the first thing to ask **for is His Kingdom to come,** *and* **His will to be done.**

Asking for God's Kingdom to come is the beginning of seeking His Kingdom, and asking for His will to be *done* on earth the way it is done in heaven is seeking His righteousness.

The righteousness of God is, in a sense, the will of God. What God wants is what is right. Whatever God will have as right is what is acceptable as right. Whatever God decides is right, is right.

To know what God deems right, we ought to read and study the

Bible. The Bible is the written Word of God. If God were to say anything to you, it would already be in the Bible right now.

In chapter 15 of the first book of Samuel, God gave King Saul clear instructions to carry out, but he did otherwise. Saul believed that saving the best things to sacrifice to the Lord was the most appropriate thing to do; after all it was God who gave them the victory, so He deserved it. But by God's standards, the most appropriate thing to do was to utterly destroy *everyone* and *everything* as He commanded.

Because of this, Saul was rejected by God. He was plagued by evil spirits, the kingdom was taken from him, and his life ended sadly. (See 1 Samuel 28-31.) Through the years he reigned, he had sought to expand God's chosen kingdom, Israel. He had sought the Kingdom of God, but without seeking His righteousness it all came to naught.

In this story, we see the will of man against the will of God. What Saul saw as a job well done, God saw as rebellion and disobedience. Saul thought he had finished his work but by God's standards, he had done the wrong thing.

Sometimes, God gives us an instruction, but we think we know better. The route that looks right to us seems socially acceptable, just as the choice Saul made was favoured by the people he ruled, but this doesn't make it right in God's eyes. It is important to do what is right by God, and not what we think is right, even when it doesn't seem to make sense.

"For as the heavens are higher than the earth, so are my ways higher than your ways, and my thoughts higher than your thoughts."

- Isaiah 55:9

DOING THE RIGHT THING

"If any man will do his will, he shall know of the doctrine, whether it be of God or whether I speak of myself."

-John 7:17

The result of your activities will prove whether you are in God's will. God only reveals His plans to those who believe enough to act on what He has said.

You will always know when you have done what God wants, though you will only know that you have done it right when you have finished doing it. This is where the just must live by faith.

Hardly ever do you know how good you are in any subject until you have been tested on it. Oftentimes, people who are the most confident that they know a lot on a particular topic find out that they did not actually know as much as they thought they did. Doing God's will is important because it is what will determine whether you walk in the Kingdom of God. It is what determines if you go to heaven.

Heaven can only be entered by those who attain to God's standards of doing right, and those who do so achieve this by applying a considerable amount of effort. They *violently* take it *by force*. This doesn't mean we are justified by our works; it means we get to heaven by having faith in God enough to live by what He says is right.

It takes something extra to attain to God's standards and if we do not apply a considerable amount of force, we are bound to fall short. Jesus always talked about the will of God when he talked about heaven, and he always showed that doing it was a major (and usually the only) criteria for entering heaven.

> *"Wherefore by their fruits ye shall know them. Not everyone that saith unto me, Lord, Lord, shall enter into the kingdom of heaven: but he that doeth the will of my father which is in heaven."*
>
> -Matthew 7:20-21

JUSTIFICATION BY FAITH

"Now faith is ... the evidence of things not seen."

-Hebrews 11:1

When God sees someone as righteous, He looks at what they have done in every situation and says, "They did the right thing." For God to say, "Well done," it means you have met His standards, you have done the right thing by Him, you have attained His righteousness. (See Matthew 25:21.)

This is what is known as justification.

For God to justify you, it means He is defending your actions. It means He sees what you have done as the right thing and actually has proof to back up His claim. And the proof God uses is your faith.

Believing and acting on God's Word reveals faith in Him. If you truly believe the Word of God, you will act on it. People may condemn you and your actions but, in the eyes of God, you are righteous. The explanation for your behaviour is your obedience to His instruction, and that is the definition of doing the right thing by Him.

THE FAITH OF ABEL

"By faith Abel offered unto God a more excellent sacrifice than Cain, by which he obtained witness that he was righteous, God testifying of his gifts: and by it he being dead yet speaketh"

-Hebrews 11:4

Abel offered a more excellent sacrifice than his brother, Cain, because he believed in something. Therefore, God said he had done well. This was why God bore witness that he was righteous.

Righteousness doesn't come by believing in any random thing. It comes by faith in God, by believing in Jesus who is The Living Word of God. Jesus had not yet come in the time of Cain and Abel which meant that the only Word of God they had was in spoken form.

God still fellowshipped with Adam and his family after they got thrown out of the Garden of Eden, but it was not as before.

When we read Genesis 4:1-12, we see that as time passed, Cain and Abel decide to offer up a sacrifice to God. Up until this point, since the creation of man, there had been no mention of any law or instruction to follow about giving an offering to God.

Cain was clearly hardworking. He was a tiller of the ground and that is really hard work: to break ground, cultivate it, plant fruit, nurture it, and then harvest it. Cain offered some of his fruits and Abel offered some of his firstlings, and both their offerings were excellent. Abel's was considered more excellent by God, and the writer of Hebrews tells us this is so because his offering was an act of faith.

God did not pronounce curses on Adam and Eve because He was angry, He simply told them the consequences of their actions… **But that was not His will for them!** When Adam and Eve fell to the curse, it did not nullify God's words or instructions; it just meant that it would be harder for them to keep to, not impossible.

The Lord made man so he could replenish the earth and subdue it. God made man to take care of the earth and make everything increase.

My belief (and you can take this with a pinch—or spoonful—of salt) is that Cain chose to break the ground because it was what he saw his father doing. After all, he was the first child, so he would learn his father's trade and God had sent Adam out of the Garden to till the ground for food because of his disobedience.

Understand that tilling the earth is not wrong. It is also a process to make it fruitful. There would have been no way to eat or feed sheep without the earth being tilled, yet God still told Cain that he did not do well—he did not act according to the will of God, despite his excellent sacrifice.

It is my belief that Abel walked by faith in God and built on his relationship with the Lord enough so that he offered his firstlings, probably all he had at the time. I believe even Abel's choice of what to become (a keeper of sheep) was influenced by his knowledge of and relationship with God.

Abel knew God loved him. He understood why God had made him and he believed in the will of God for his life. God had made him to keep.

Cain, on the other hand, walked by sight. He put his faith in the consequences of his father's actions and not entirely in the Words of God, so God did not regard his offering and did not think what he was doing was the right thing.

Doing well here is according to God's standard and no one else's. In God's eyes, Abel did well and Cain did not, and the difference was due to Abel's faith and Cain's lack thereof.

RUBY WAS RESTORED

Years ago, I bought a pair of mini speakers to listen to music out loud on my silver Sony Walkman because the two were going together at a bargain price. I found out later that this was so because it was an old model, and it could not rewind or fast-forward.

After a few years, a friend of mine borrowed my Walkman and when they returned it, they informed me that it had mysteriously died. I really liked that Walkman and tried to get it fixed but all my attempts were futile.

I couldn't play my music anymore because it was broken so I decided to replace it since it could no longer serve the function for which it was bought. I, however, kept it and the speakers.

A few weeks later, I bought a red and black Sony Walkman and this one could both rewind and fast-forward, it even had an auto repeat function! I named her Ruby because she was such a gem to me.

I tried my speakers from my previous Walkman on her and they worked perfectly until one day, another friend borrowed Ruby and when he returned her, she too had mysteriously died. I was so upset about this but because I loved Ruby so much, I couldn't bear to throw her away.

I kept her and I tried every way I could to revive her, but it was pointless. I resorted to the last possible thing I could think of. I prayed. I asked God to please bring Ruby back to life, and then I put her safe in my electro box (an old sweet-tin where I keep bits and bobs from old electronic devices) and left her there.

One random day, when I was clearing out my electro box, I stumbled upon Ruby and my silver Sony Walkman which couldn't rewind or fast-forward. I decided to test them one last time, so I plugged in the silver Walkman. It didn't work, so I threw it away. I tried Ruby and to my amazement, she worked!

From that day, I restored her to her position of my favourite listening device. You see, the fact that she stopped working for a while did not change the reason for which I bought her, and I was ready to restore her to her former state if she started functioning again. However, I threw away my silver Walkman because it could no longer perform the function for which it was bought.

Because you may have made mistakes in the past, because you may have stopped functioning, it doesn't change the reason for which God created you.

God is willing and ready to restore you if only you would rise and begin to function again in the role for which he called you. You will however be thrown out if you fail to function after countless opportunities to do so.

★★★

Because you have sinned does not nullify or change the reason why God made you or called you. And being righteous and truly holy is living out that will and fulfilling that purpose. God gave them the earth to keep.

God has given everyone something and He expects us to keep it, be it a commandment or a ministry, His command is to *keep* what He has given us. God gave Jesus his sheep and Jesus kept them. God wants people who will keep whatever it is He gives them.

Faith in God is proven by keeping His commandments. Doing this

THY WILL BE DONE

will mean you act in a certain way to do what he says, and when you do, God will approve of your behaviour.

> "Not every one that saith unto me, Lord, Lord, shall enter into the kingdom of heaven; but he that doeth the will of my Father which is in heaven."
>
> -Matthew 7:21

THE WAY

"He made known his ways unto Moses, his acts unto the children of Israel."

-Psalms 103:7

I have come to realise that it is not just about knowing *what* God wants but also understanding *how* He plans to achieve it.

The way God does things is very different from the way we as humans do things. Saying "I surrender," is not just giving in to what God wants, but also the way He wants it done.

Moses was special to God. Moses was His friend. God showed Moses how He did things. He showed all of Israel what He did, but Moses knew more than just His will, Moses knew His ways. You might know what God wants you to do but you must also endeavour to find out how He wants it done.

Often, we are so concerned about the "do" that we do not take the time to find out "how" the "do" is meant to be done.

This is where wisdom and understanding come in.

Wisdom put simply is doing the right thing at the right time.

When we listen to an instruction, we learn what to do and when to do it. When we *understand* the instruction, we learn how to do it. It's pretty simple. When I was in school, we were taught formulae for solving different equations.

Our teachers knew that if we understood how the formula worked, we would end up at the right answer so, for example, we were taught that the formula for finding the area of a circle is $A = \pi r^2$.

Knowing this formula does not guarantee that you could find the area of any given circle, but being made to understand that:

- π is a constant with the value 22/7 or 3.14,
- r is the radius of the circle
- the radius of a circle is half the diameter of the circle

This made it possible for us to apply the formula effectively and solve problems when only the diameter of the circle was given and even solve problems in reverse such as finding the diameter of the circle with the same formula when only the area was given.

It is much easier to do things when you understand how they are meant to be done. Much frustration comes not only from doing the wrong things, but also from doing the right things in the wrong way.

There is a particular way to do things and most of the time; your success in doing something is determined by how it is done. The same thing applies to the will of God.

That is why Solomon, the wisest man to ever live, recorded that wisdom is the main thing to get, but while you are learning what to do, make sure you learn *how* to do it.

To know how God works, we must understand how He thinks and to do that, we need to know Him on a personal level, just as Moses did.

Righteous people are not those who are too busy doing everything or those who just stand still doing nothing, they are those who do what God tells them to do. When you know me on a personal level, you will know exactly how I like my coffee.

When we know God on a personal level, He will tell us what He wants and how He wants it whenever we ask Him.

"Wisdom is the principal thing; therefore get wisdom: and with all thy getting get understanding."

-Proverbs 4:7

GROWING IN GOD

"And the child grew; and waxed strong in spirit, filled with wisdom: and the grace of God was upon him."

-Luke 2:40

As a child, prophecies went forth about Jesus... but, like I said, he was only a child. So how could he possibly have known or understood these things when his parents clearly did not?

After the prophecies given at his presentation, the first thing we see Jesus doing is growing.

To grow means to undergo natural development by increasing in size and changing physically. It is to become larger or greater over a period. Growth means increase.

Jesus did not only grow physically. This passage is also talking about spiritual growth and maturity, as it states that he "waxed strong *in spirit...*"

He grew and developed spiritually, becoming larger or greater over a period, as he increased and was *filled with wisdom*. He matured spiritually, and *the grace of God was upon him*.

This is how Jesus knew the will of God for his life. He was filled with the spirit of wisdom and understanding, he had the grace of God, but none of his great works came until *after* he grew.

Jesus is a living example of how to grow spiritually. When he told his parents that he must be about his Father's business, they did not understand. They did not understand that his staying behind at the temple to learn and ask questions was him being about his Father's business.

God's business (will) for him at that time was to grow and be anointed, and that meant waiting behind and doing whatever it would take to grow in the knowledge of God.

"As new born babes, desire the sincere milk of the Word, that ye may grow thereby."

-1 Peter 2:2

SEASONS

"To everything there is a season, and a time to every purpose under the heaven."

-Ecclesiastes 3:1

There are different seasons in life and, as mentioned in the previous chapter, the first of them is where God has ordained that we grow and wax *strong in spirit*. Missing the opportunities presented in one season can affect every other aspect and season in your life.

God has ordained that you achieve specific things in each season. This is not disregarding grace for a second and third chance, but missing out on what God has ordained for you to achieve in a particular season can—and oftentimes, does—have a ripple effect on the rest of your life.

In Luke 2, Jesus was in the time or season where he needed one to teach him because he was as such that had need of milk. The first principles of the oracles of God are the first basic truths or laws by which God has established for His oracles to be carried out.

The way He has established is that first, you need milk to grow so you need to be fed with it the way a new-born babe has to be fed because they cannot feed themselves—you need *a teacher*.

After that, the next principle is that you grow up by exercising your senses in discerning good and evil. Then you go on to teach others. This is the strong meat referred to in Hebrews 5:12-14.

Learn what season you are in and walk worthy of it because there is a time slot apportioned to everything God has called you to do. To walk righteously is to do what has called you to do, the way He has called you to do it, *when* He calls you to do it because His will for one season is not always His will for another.

That you do not know the will of God for your life shows that you still need one to teach, guide and direct you. You cannot go running off to *do* God's will when you do not even know what you are meant to be doing.

If you are not prepared, when you get to the battle, you will not be skilled in using your weapons and you will most probably get killed. What will keep your feet steady and allow you to stand when the attack comes is how well you prepared for it.

"And your feet shod with the preparation of the gospel of peace."

-Ephesians 6:15

DIFFERENT SEASONS OF LIFE

"To every thing there is a season, and a time to every purpose under the heaven:"

- Ecclesiastes 3:1

God doesn't give many complicated instructions all at once, He just gives 1 and He gives you a *time frame* to do it in. This time frame is called a *season*. There are many seasons in the Bible because there are many instructions God gives to many.

A few of these seasons are mentioned in different parts of the Bible, but are listed in Ecclesiastes 3:2-8.

1. The season of birth
2. The season of death
3. The season to plant
4. The season of harvest
5. The season to kill
6. The season of healing
7. The season to break down
8. The season to build up

9. The season of weeping
10. The season of laughter
11. The season of mourning
12. The season of dancing
13. The season for casting away stones
14. The season of gathering stones together
15. The season of embracing
16. The season of refraining from embracing
17. The season to get
18. The season to lose
19. The season to keep
20. The season to cast away
21. The season to rent
22. The season to sew
23. The season to keep silent
24. The season to speak
25. The season to love
26. The season to hate
27. The season of war
28. The season of peace

These are at least 28 different seasons for 28 different activities God has for you to carry out or experience. There are many seasons in this life and the first season is always *birth*.

In John 12:24, Jesus describes our fruit-bearing process, and he describes us as seeds.

We are Christ's fruit—this is the season of being born again, the stage where we came on the scene.

The next stage is where the fruit itself is eaten and the seed is left bare and naked. After that, the seed has to fall to the ground and unless the seed falls to the ground *and dies*, it cannot bring forth fruit.

The seed stays in the ground for a time; it begins to develop *roots* and the roots begin to sink deeper and deeper into the soil before the shoot starts to come forth, grow, and then bear fruit.

FOUR STAGES OF LIFE AND MINISTRY

"Be glad then, ye children of Zion, and rejoice in the Lord your God: for he hath given you the former rain moderately, and he will cause to come down for you the rain, the former rain, and the latter rain in the first month."

-Joel 2:23

Every Christian's life and ministry is divided into four stages but not everyone completes all of them and that is why Jesus was so keen on finishing the work he had been given. (See John 4:34, 17:4.)

STAGE ONE: THE EARLY RAIN STAGE

As the early rains come, the ground gets soft and good for planting. This is when seeds are sown, when one becomes born again and begins to build their Christian foundations.

In the book of John 3:3, the phrase "born again" is translated from the Greek, *"gennethe anothen,"* which refers to a transformation from God and a renewal in righteousness and true holiness to be saved.

To be fully conformed to Christ's image, the Holy Spirit comes to dwell within, teach, and reveal Christ to the believer. This seals the believer as God's own.

STAGE TWO: AFTER THE EARLY RAIN

After the planting is done, the seeds begin to germinate. Roots sink deep as the seed cap peels off. This is the time in the life of a Christian where one's heart is circumcised, where one develops roots which sink deep into God and His Word.

This is when many hear *the call* of God. God calls you out and sets you apart **to be pruned and prepared** for His special purpose.

This calling and setting apart can be referred to as a special sort of anointing. It is the anointing David received in 1 Samuel 16:11-13. This anointing is the Hebrew word "*Mashyach*."

This is when God takes the called through fire and tries them like gold. God will call you and watch how faithful you are through different tests before He chooses to bestow great power on you. The power of God comes with great responsibility, and the tests prove (to Him, yourself and the world) you are worthy to be trusted with it.

There is a price for the call of God, a separation and sanctification and purification of one's heart, desires, and intentions. Oftentimes, this occurs through the fiery tests of life and circumstance. But no one receives the power of the Holy Ghost until they have passed these tests.

SIX DIMENSIONS OF THE MASHYACH ANOINTING

Here are six features of the call of God to be set aside in preparation for His work and power. This is not an exhaustive list of signs, symptoms, or what to expect when one is called, it is, however, common to experience one or more of these when one is called.

1. Being marked as special

> *"But against any of the children of Israel shall not a dog move his tongue, against man or beast: that ye may know how that the LORD doth put a difference between the Egyptians and Israel."*
>
> -Exodus 11:7

The hand of God on a person's life sets them apart. And it is easy for that person to be seen as special, for their gifts to become more apparent and, because of the changes in their character during the pruning, for them to seem different.

It is also common to experience favour from those in authority, and to be helped in inexplicable ways. This is because your focus as one who is being tested is to pass the test and grow into what God has called you to be.

Any distractions get taken care of.

2. Being changed

> *"That saith, I will build me a wide house and large chambers, and cutteth him out windows; and it is ceiled with cedar, and painted with vermilion."*
>
> *-Jeremiah 22:14*

Times of testing produce changes. When God calls someone to be tested and purified, imperfections in character are stripped away. A person seems better, improved.

The person is changed.

Oftentimes, these changes make one noticeable. Likeable, even. When one is raised by God and becomes noticeable, it is not a thing to be taken lightly. Remember, this is a time of testing, and there is still much to learn, much to develop into after being anointed.

God will lead His anointed through situations that will mellow and mature them. These are *"shadow of death"* situations which inspire faith and complete confidence in God. Simply hearing the call and being called anointed doesn't turn you into something you are not. Being anointed requires *being changed*. It requires becoming someone with complete faith and trust in God. And that requires work.

3. Being plagued with battles

> *"Prepare the table, watch in the watchtower, eat, drink: arise, ye*

princes, and anoint the shield."

-Isaiah 21:5

Troubles often are a sign that one has been called by God. Fire must be hot enough to burn imperfections if it is to purify.

When one is marked out by God, they often become a target for agents of darkness. God will never allow you to face more that you can handle, but He will definitely allow you have *something* to handle. And to mature, handle it, you must.

Amidst the eating and drinking and preparing for the power and blessings of God that come with being chosen, one must also prepare for the attacks it brings. A lighthouse is a beacon for *anyone* out at sea. Both fishermen and pirates see the light.

Jeremiah, one of the greatest prophets to ever walk the earth, was a very, very, *very* troubled man.

4. Being able to minister

"And this is the thing that thou shalt do unto them to hallow them, to minister unto me in the priests office: Take one young bullock, and two rams without blemish, and unleavened bread, and cakes unleavened tempered with oil, and wafers unleavened anointed with oil: of wheaten flour shalt thou make them."

-Exodus 29:1-2

Ministration isn't screaming and turning and falling about the place.

Ministration isn't necessarily smearing things or people with oil. It isn't just preaching from a pulpit or singing to a congregation.

Ministration is providing care and assistance to God's people, when and how it is needed. Speaking words of encouragement to one person is ministration as much as preaching to masses on stage is. It is also providing care.

One who is anointed and is growing in the Word and knowledge of God, one who is changing and being purified, will minister to those around them, even without realising. This is because they are being forged into a vessel God can use to reach and care for His people.

God ministers to and through those He has called.

5. Being appointed to an office

> *"And the Lord said unto him, Go, return on thy way to the wilderness of Damascus: and when thou comest, anoint Hazael to be king over Syria: and Jehu the son of Nimshi shalt thou anoint to be king over Israel: and Elisha the son of Shaphat of Abel-meholah shalt thou anoint to be a prophet in thy room."*
>
> *-1 Kings 19:15-16*

The mashyach anointing is a calling in preparation for what God has for you. And sometimes, this preparation includes being appointed to specific roles or offices.

It is not strange to find oneself being put in positions of authority and responsibility. However significant, or insignificant, the role may be, being called upon to occupy a position of authority often occurs when one has been marked by God.

6. Becoming a vessel unto honour

> *"Before I formed thee in the belly I knew thee; and before thou camest forth out of the womb I sanctified thee, and I ordained thee a prophet unto the nations."*
>
> -Jeremiah 1:5

It is possible to be called and go on to become a vessel God uses without even realising it. It is possible to have been purged, pruned, and purified without having the slightest clue. This is often due to a lack of understanding, and results in people saying things like "God worked it all out for my good." (Yeah, I know it is a scripture.)

Without guidance and understanding, it is easy to feel like life is just happening to you when it's actually happening for you, like everything is falling apart when it's actually falling into place. God orders our steps in every season of our lives; He tests and purifies and moulds those He calls. And it is very possible that He called and tested and moulded you into the vessel you are without you knowing it was happening.

Jeremiah was called and sanctified to be a prophet long before God ever spoke to him. Moses was trained in Pharaoh's palace and spent 40 years living in desert before his encounter with the burning bush.

And all that was to prepare him to lead the people of Israel to the promised land.

STAGE THREE: THE LATTER RAIN

This would be the season in the development of a plant where its shoot begins to appear. For a Christian, this is when one emerges from obscurity and starts functioning in the office God has called them to.

In this fledgling season of ministry, one settles into their role, into their calling. One learns the nuances of ministry and finds their place in the world. Just as any plant in this fledgling season, one needs water and sunlight and, most importantly, protection.

> *"Wherefore take unto you the whole armour of God, that ye may be able to withstand in the evil day, and having done all, to stand."*
>
> *-Ephesians 6:13*

This is the season one learns to put on the whole armour of God—the protection provided by God—and follow the leading of the Holy Spirit.

> *"For the prophecy came not in old time by the will of man: but holy men of God spake as they were moved by the Holy Ghost."*
>
> *-2 Peter 1:21*

STAGE FOUR: AFTER THE LATTER RAIN

"But ye shall receive power, after that the Holy Ghost is come upon

you and ye shall be witnesses unto me both in Jerusalem, and in all Judea, and in Samaria, and unto the uttermost part of the earth."

-Acts 1:8

The time of harvest has come, the fruit is ripe and ready for picking. This ripeness speaks of maturity. When one has learned to identify the leading of the Holy Ghost and has become comfortable in their armour and skilled in using their weapons, they are spiritually mature. (See Ephesians 6:13-17.)

This is the point at which one is expected to bear fruit.

The beginning of this season is marked by the outpouring of the Holy Ghost. The word "Power" in the above verse is the Greek word, "*Dunamis.*" Before God sends one out into ministry, one must first receive the Dunamis Anointing. This anointing is for explosive growth, and this growth and expansion takes place in four parts. I have termed them according to the verse for easier understanding.

Part One: The First Set

This is being a minister to your inner core. This is where the anointing upon your life affects those closest to you. For the disciples in Jerusalem, this meant a sphere of influence (or being a witness) in Jerusalem.

Part Two: The Second Set

This is ministering to those outside your inner circle but still inside your comfort zone. In the verse, the anointing the disciples received would make them witnesses not only in Jerusalem, but it would also extend their influence to Judea.

Part Three: The Fringes

Consider this to be ministering to those you normally would have no dealings with. The Jews had little to do with the Samaritans, but when the Holy Ghost was poured out on them, their influence was to extend even to these people on the outskirts.

Part Four: The Beyond

Named so, partly because I am a fantasy writer and as such, have a flare for the dramatic. The Beyond simply means beyond borders. This level of ministry goes beyond both physical and metaphorical boundaries to reach those further than your imagination ever thought you would.

REWARDS OF RIGHTEOUSNESS

"Behold, the righteous shall be recompensed in the earth..."

-Proverbs 11:31

There is a reward for righteousness. There are many rewards, actually. It is all but impossible to walk in the will of God and not see benefits or reap rewards. Even the peace of mind that comes with knowing one is in the will of God can be considered a reward.

The word "recompense" means "to pay or reward for effort or work." Jesus said in Matthew 5:6, "*Blessed* are they which do hunger and thirst after righteousness: for they shall be filled."

Here are some rewards for doing the will of God:

1. God's wisdom *(Proverbs 2:7)*
2. Being special to God *(Proverbs 3:32)*
3. Being loved by God *(Psalms 146:8)*
4. Divine protection *(Proverbs 18:10)*
5. Deliverance *(Psalms 34:19)*
6. Answered prayers *(Proverbs 15:29)*
7. Favour *(Psalms 5:12)*

8. Righteous people are known by God *(Psalms 1:6)*
9. The presence of God *(Psalms 14:5)*
10. Establishment *(Psalms 55:22)*
11. An earthly inheritance *(Psalms 37:29)*
12. Joy and gladness *(Psalms 64:10)*
13. Growth and development *(Psalms 92:12)*
14. Continuity *(Jeremiah 23:5)*
15. Fulfilled desires *(Proverbs 10:24)*
16. Knowledge *(Proverbs 10:32)*
17. Fruitfulness and abundance *(Proverbs 12:12)*
18. Satisfaction *(Proverbs 13:25)*
19. Exaltation *(Psalms 75:10)*
20. Riches and treasures *(Proverbs 15:6)*
21. The hope of eternal life *(Proverbs 14:32)*
22. Direction *(Proverbs 15:19)*
23. Sustenance *(Psalms 55:22)*
24. Support *(Proverbs 28:12)*
25. Wellness *(Isaiah 3:10)*
26. Entry into heaven *(Psalms 118:20)*

THE PATH OF RIGHTEOUSNESS

"There is a way which seemeth right unto a man, but the end thereof are the ways of death."

– Proverbs 14:12

King Solomon, the wisest man that ever lived, wrote books on wisdom. In one, he compiled his father's teachings on life and wisdom, including things like what to do, where to go, and who to associate with. This book is known as Proverbs.

One thing often touched on in this book is the right path to take. Solomon mentioned that the paths of righteousness were ones his father advised were the best to keep to. In the second chapter of Proverbs, he mentions a number of paths, and separates them into two categories: the paths wisdom will lead him on, and the paths wisdom will lead him off.

"... wide is the gate, and broad is the way, that leadeth to destruction... strait is the gate, and narrow is the way, which leadeth unto life, and few there be that find it."

-Matthew 7:13-14

These two paths, which to stay on and which to get off, are determined by their destinations. No matter what paths one decides to walk in this life, all roads lead to one of two places in the end.

1. The paths that lead to death

> *"For her house inclineth unto death, and her paths unto the dead."*
>
> *– Proverbs 2:18*

2. The paths that lead to life

> *"But small is the gate and narrow is the road that leads to life, and only few find it.."*
>
> *– Matthew 7:14 (New International Version)*

★★★

THE PATHS OF DEATH

The paths of death are the paths that lead to sheol and destruction.

So, if you pull a Kevin McCallister and hop on down a route without checking its destination, one way to tell what path you're on (according to Solomon and his father) is to take a look at your companions. Those easily spotted on the paths of death include:

1. The evil man

> *"To deliver thee from the way of the evil man..."*
>
> *– Proverbs 2:12*

Some people are evil by a universal standard. There's no argument as to the subjective nature of right and wrong in their situation. These aren't morally grey characters in the books we read, the kind we hope would have a redemption arc.

They're just plain evil.

To be on the same path as such a person is a sign that one is going the wrong way.

2. The froward speaking man

> *"... from the man that speaketh forward things."*
>
> *– Proverbs 2:12*

This is one who habitually speaks of disobedience and opposition. It speaks of someone who is rebellious and difficult to deal with. A froward person is difficult to control, someone who habitually opposes authority by the way they behave and the things they say.

Here's the interesting part: Solomon advises we steer clear of those who speak like that. This means those who grumble and talk of rebellion. They might not be doing it yet, but even speaking about it tells you what path they're headed down.

3. The Man of Darkness

> *"Those who leave the paths of uprightness, to walk in the ways of darkness;"*
>
> *– Proverbs 2:13*

Have you ever tried to find your way across a dark cluttered room? You will never make it from one end to the other without hurting yourself in some way. Plus, there is always that fear that something is lurking in the darkness and the assurance that you will bump into something.

Now, imagine one who thrives in such conditions. There are those who walk in darkness, those whose deeds cannot be done in daylight. Being on the same path as one who constantly must hide their actions because of the unsavoury nature of their deeds is a sure sign you're headed the wrong way.

4. The crooked man

"Whose ways are crooked and they froward in their paths:"

– Proverbs 2:15

Those who walk in deception and dishonesty walk a crooked, shady path. They are easy to spot, and once you do, avoid them.

Turn around. Run. Get away.

Once entangled with such people, it is difficult to get free from them or the destruction that awaits them.

THE PATHS OF LIFE

We've looked at a few lanes on the highway to hell. Now, here are a few paths mentioned in the Bible leading on to heaven:

1. The paths of judgement

> "He keepeth the paths of judgment..."
>
> *—Proverbs 2:8*

Judgement speaks about the ability to assess situations or circumstances shrewdly and to draw sound conclusions. It takes wisdom and knowledge to be able to make sound decisions.

2. The way of the saints

> "He... preserveth the way of his saints."
>
> *—Proverbs 2:8*

The saints are the called of God, those who walk in the way of the Lord, and gather together to serve Him.

3. The paths of the righteous

> "That thou mayest walk in the way of good men, and keep the paths of the righteous"
>
> *—Proverbs 2:20*

Those who walk in uprightness are those who walk honestly and straightforward.

4. The way of good men

> "That thou mayest walk in the way of good men, and keep the paths of the righteous"
>
> *—Proverbs 2:20*

HE LEADETH ME

"The LORD is my shepherd; I shall not want. He maketh me to lie down in green pastures: he leadeth me beside the still waters. He restoreth my soul: he leadeth me in the paths of righteousness for his name's sake."

-Psalms 23:1-3

One blessing of being a child of God is that God leads you down the paths of righteousness. The Lord leads everyone who is called by His name and does so by His Holy Spirit.

"For as many as are led by the Spirit of God, they are the sons of God."

– Romans 8:14

THREE REASONS WHY WE MUST BE LED DOWN THE PATHS OF RIGHTEOUSNESS

1. The road is narrow, and it is difficult to find

"Because strait is the gate, and narrow is the way, which leadeth unto life, and few there be that find it."

–Matthew 7:14

2. There are many afflictions on the way

"Many are the afflictions of the righteous: but the Lord delivereth him out of them all."

-Psalms 34:19

3. It is a violent road

> *"And from the days of John the Baptist until now the kingdom of heaven suffereth violence, and the violent take it by force."*
>
> —Matthew 11:12

FOR HIS NAME'S SAKE

"Let not your heart be troubled: ye believe in God, believe also in me. In my Father's house are many mansions: if it were not so, I would have told you. I go to prepare a place for you. And if I go and prepare a place for you, I will come again, and receive you unto myself; that where I am, there ye may be also. And wither I go ye know, and the way ye know."

-John 14:1-4

When Jesus went on to eternal life, he told his disciples that they knew the way to where he would be. We have seen that the path of righteousness is the path to eternal life, so it is safe to infer that the way to eternal life is the path of righteousness.

Jesus is saying we know the path of righteousness, although few people actually find it (Matthew 7:14). But most don't know and can't identify this path. The disciples felt much the same when he told them this truth.

It is true that a lot of believers think they do not know and cannot identify this path to righteousness, so they walk a tightrope of laws to govern their own lives in the belief that the "narrow way" means "restrictions" and "bondage to the law," but this is not so.

When one comes to know God, one is no longer under the law, one lives under the grace of God. Jesus came to set us free from bondage, not to bind us up some more. If Jesus says we know the way to where he is, then we definitely know the way.

We may not know it is the way or know it as the way that it is, but we definitely know this way that leads to eternal life. That way is Jesus.

"Jesus saith unto him, I am the way, the truth, and the life: no man cometh unto the father, but by me."

—John 14:6

Jesus is the way to eternal life. Jesus is the path of righteousness that leads to the Father. Jesus leads you in the path of righteous by his Holy Spirit because you are called by his name. Because you know him, you know the way to eternal life. Because you know him, you will always know what God wants you to do and how He wants you to do it.

Because you know him, not as a man, but as the son of the living God, you will live righteously and inherit eternal life.

That is why every believer has been given the Holy Spirit. The Holy Spirit bears witness to this and leads the believer to be with God, the way a one takes the hand of a lost child and leads them back home again.

CHASING GOD

BEGINNING WITH SALVATION

"But seek ye first the kingdom of God, and his righteousness; and all these things shall be added unto you."

- Matthew 6:33

A journey of a thousand miles begins with one step, and the first step on this journey is what Jesus calls being *born again*.

Many people have different understandings of what it means to be born again. Books have been written and messages preached extensively on this topic because many people still do not know what it means. In this book, the definition of the term "born again" is taken from what Jesus said, it is being born of water and of the Spirit.

This concept is explained more extensively in *Understanding Christianity*.

There are few things I would like to stress here as we begin our journey of finding God:

1. You must be born again

Being born again is not an option on this journey, it is a requirement. If we want to enter the Kingdom of God, or even see it, we need to be born again. We need to be created anew, born of water and of the Spirit.

2. Starting the journey isn't equivalent to finishing it

Being born again lets us see the kingdom of God, but it does not guarantee entrance into it. This journey to finding God is lifelong and beginning it does not automatically guarantee that you will reach the destination. Therefore, it is very important to stay the course once begun till the very end.

3. You need the Holy Spirit

Being born again is about the spirit life and, as Jesus explained, it is the Holy Spirit who gives birth to the spirit life. Without the Holy Spirit, one can neither be born again, nor be a true Christian.

A PERSONAL FOUNDATION

Three key habits to develop in order to lay a good personal foundation for one's Christian walk, are the habits of prayer, quiet time, and fellowship.

Prayer

The presence of God to a Christian is like water to a fish, prayer as our gills, and faith, the oxygen we extract.

Prayer is nothing short of spiritual breathing. We need it to survive, and yet, like breathing, we sometimes forget its importance until our bodies begin to shut down for lack of oxygen. The only difference is, we sometimes fail to realise that the shutting down of our spiritual lives is due to a lack of prayer.

Prayer in its most basic form is communication with God.

Relationships are built on communication and without this key ingredient, any relationship is bound to wither and eventually die. In our new or renewed relationship with Christ, it is important that we begin to pray regularly.

There are different types of prayer and different extensive teachings on it, such as those of E. M. Bounds and Smith Wigglesworth. I recommend such teachings for further study about prayer.

Quiet Time

A quiet time is the intimate time you spend alone with God, in His presence and in His Word. Quiet time consists of reading the Bible and studying the word through commentaries and devotionals, reflection on the Word, and meditation. This is the time one often hears from God and gets to know Him.

A book that would help in learning how to have an effective quiet time is *Quiet Time,* by Dag Heward-Mills.

Fellowship

Fellowship is important in our growth and walk as Christians because when we gather in God's name, He has promised to be there in our midst.

Also, when we meet in fellowship, we share the Word of God to receive correction, encouragement, and direction for our lives.

If you have not already done so, it would be good to find a Bible-based church to commit to and share fellowship with.

FROM A BACKGROUND OF NOTHINGNESS

"And they took them wives of the women of Moab; the name of the one was Orpah, and the name of the other Ruth..."

-Ruth 1:4

Ruth, like us, was an outsider. A Moabite who served different gods, just like us, became grafted onto the family tree of Christ. It is only befitting that we learn from her example seeing as we are in no different a predicament than she was. (See Ruth 1.)

The first lesson that we can learn, coming from a background of nothingness into a royal priesthood is this: **your story did not begin with you.**

This is a point I will continue to stress as we go along our journey as it is something so important and yet so simple that a lot of people trivialize it to their own detriment.

In looking at the story of Ruth, we, like the Bible, will start at the beginning, before she even entered the picture.

★★★

BEGINNING FROM THE START

Life was hard in Israel because there was a famine. A famine represents lack, barrenness, and an inability to bring forth. A famine is a hopeless situation in which many people perish. There was a famine and because of this, a certain man made a decision to take himself, his wife, and his sons away to find greener pastures.

This man's name was Elimelech.

Elimelech, who later became Ruth's father-in-law, took Naomi, Malhon and Chilion from their home and their country in order to ensure their survival in a difficult situation.

I would like to draw our attention to the truth that sometimes, we end up in a place, not because of our decisions, but because of the decisions of those over and above us. We must understand that the reason we exist today is because of decisions made by our fathers, be it spiritual or physical.

Elimelech was the father who took the decision which led to Ruth's open door, and though without him, this story would probably have turned out differently, it is very easy to neglect his impact on the situation because he was already dead before Ruth came into the picture.

There are fathers taking decisions which are impacting our lives. We must not neglect them. Remember that your story did not begin with you.

FOUR LESSONS FOR THE JOURNEY

1. Decisions are powerful

Big decisions bring about big changes. Little decisions bring about little changes which, in time, could grow to have great effect. A difference of one degree in direction may look little at the start, but after a considerable distance, one would find they may be thrown completely off the mark.

Elimelech made a hard decision to bring about drastic change in the lives of his family members and, after making this journey, he died. In need of a drastic change, he made a serious decision which affected others. If we were to count the people who were directly affected by the decision to leave Israel, we would have himself, Naomi, Malhon and Chilion (his two sons), Ruth and Orpah along with their families, Boaz and his household to name a few.

From this example, we can see in the far-reaching consequences of Elimelech's decision, that a decision is a very powerful thing. *Thus, your decision to chase after God will not only affect you, but many others around you along the way.* It is very important that we be mindful of this, to avoid being startled or confused by the possible effects when we start to see them.

2. You will lose relationships

When we begin our journey to the presence of God, He will use many different people to impact us at different stages of our lives. Some will remain with us, while others will be taken out of the picture for one reason or another. When this happens, we should try to remember that not everyone has the same vision or goal as us.

Also, because we have taken a decision to chase God, there would be persons incompatible with that vision, whom we would eventually have to part ways with. These are not necessarily bad people; they are just not going where we are headed.

If you were headed to South America and your friend was headed to Africa, s/he would most probably not be getting on the same plane as you. So it is that we may also find ourselves parting company with several friends on this journey. Most of them would probably not be "bad" or "negative" influences, rather they would just not be going our way.

The life of a pilgrim is a lonely one and the sooner we come to terms with that, the easier it is for us. You may not understand this now, but with time as you continue along the journey, you will.

I have often felt lonely in my walk with God, unable to share certain secrets or experiences with those around me because I know they will not understand, but through it all, the Lord has been my comfort and I embrace and cherish the loneliness for it is in those moments that the Holy Spirit, a friend that sticks closer than a brother, is made manifest to me.

3. Your associations will change

One effect of a great decision is a change in association. Some of these changes will happen naturally as one's interests and desires begin to change, while one would need to make a conscious effort to cut some others off.

Notice how Elimelech had to make a conscious decision to change his location, which led to a change in his associations. In those days, there was no social media, email, or mobile communication for him to keep in touch with his friends back in Israel. His decision to change his location also meant a conscious decision to change his associations.

Perhaps we may not need to move cities and change our contact information, but something as little as changing the places we frequently visit or the things we do will result in a change in our associations. Choosing to seek and chase after God will result in a change in the people we relate with. When this happens, we must be spiritually minded and accept it as God's guiding hand on our lives.

Elimelech's decision to move resulted in an open door to relate with Ruth, and while it is true that Elimelech was an Israelite, of the chosen people of God, we only know his name because he was the father-in-law to Ruth, the outsider. He was the door through which she entered the lineage of Christ.

As you decide to seek God, you never know who your decision

might be opening the door to in the Kingdom.

4. Pain is a precursor to greatness

As hard as it may be to believe, pain and difficulty can direct our decisions towards God. As we see from time to time, God, in His wisdom, uses hard time such as lack (famine), discomfort (changing countries or relocating) and loss (death) to position and bring us into situations where He can do mighty things with us.

In Elimelech's hard time, he decided to move to Moab, and this resulted in his son marrying Ruth. After the two boys died, Naomi, their mother, decided in her hard time to return to Israel. Orpah, in the face of this tragedy, decided to return home to her people, but Ruth decided to stay with Naomi.

This decision that Ruth made in her pain and loyalty was probably the greatest decision she had ever made.

In our decision to walk with God, we will come across painful and difficult situations. The decisions we make in those times can be critical.

LEAVING AND CLEAVING

"... But Ruth clung tightly to Naomi..."
-Ruth1:14 (New Living Translation)

All of us have made decisions in the past; promised ourselves we would do something, or not do it, and then found ourselves going against our promise.

A common one for me is to stop eating chocolate. I like chocolate, it is a conditioned behaviour, and I honestly have no intention of giving it up completely, but I find myself wondering every New Year's Day, birthday, and any momentous occasion what it would be like to stop eating chocolate. I tell myself, "Let's try this, Xyvah! Let's see how long you can go without eating chocolate!" and then a few weeks later, I find myself buying chocolate!

This is because an idea, hope or desire to do something is different from a steadfast decision, or what some may call a *Covenant Decision*.

The Bible tells us that Ruth was determined to go with Naomi. In the King James Version, it says she was "steadfastly minded."

This is the kind of decision one does not get turned back on, no matter what comes their way. This is a decision that should not be taken lightly, a promise that must not be made on a whim.

Seeking the manifest presence of God will take more than a two-week emotionally fuelled idea, like my thoughts on what it would be like to stay away from chocolate. It takes a steadfast mind, a dedication, a covenant decision to not be turned away from seeking and chasing after the Lord. Therefore, we are required, like Ruth, to think deeply before making such a decision.

Jesus called it "counting the cost." (See Luke 14:26-33.)

COUNTING THE COST

Naomi asked both Ruth and Orpah two questions for them to think deeply on before making their decision:

"Would you therefore wait...? Would you therefore refrain from...?"
- Ruth 1:11 (English Standard Version)

These questions are posed to us who, amidst our struggles, are still seeking God. These are questions we must answer individually before we can begin the journey to finding God. Our ability to see God manifest in a certain way in our lives depends on our answers to these questions:

1. What are you ready to give up? And;
2. How long are you ready to wait?

The reality of the journey is that there is a price to pay and our ability to pay this price is dependent on our preparedness for it and our desire for our goal. It is important to think carefully about the implications of one's decision as this will help one remain steadfast along one's journey.

The price of getting a university education is not just monetary; it will cost time, energy, relationships, sleep, socialisation, leisure, entertainment, friends, and some-times even certain aspects of one's health. If one begins and is not prepared for all of these, they will struggle along the way and may eventually drop out.

There are some things to ask ourselves on this journey we have begun. Ruth looked at certain things and thought deeply about all the excuses and hurdles she anticipated she would encounter along the way. So also, we should think deeply about our answers to these questions:

1. Will distance influence your decision?
2. Will changes in your circumstances influence your decision?
3. Will difficulties influence your decision?
4. Will discomfort influence your decision?
5. Will other people and their opinions influence your decision?
6. Will the threat of death influence your decision?

COVENANT RELATIONSHIPS

"So Jonathan made a covenant with the house of David, saying, Let the LORD even require it at the hand of David's enemies."

- 1 Samuel 20:16

Relationships are very important. In our walk with God, He will bring specific people into our lives to influence the course of our destinies. These relationships are known as covenant relationships and must not be taken lightly.

As God brought Moses to Joshua, Elijah to Elisha, Saul to David and Naomi to Ruth, He will also bring a trusted person to you. Sometimes, you may think you have met them just by chance, but it is necessary to understand that with God, there is neither chance nor serendipity. God has orchestrated that relationship and your greatness will depend on your level of commitment to it.

Both Orpah and Ruth had the same relationship with Naomi, they were both her daughters-in-law. The main difference in the relationship was commitment. (See Ruth 1:6-18.)

Sometimes we may find ourselves with someone, doing the same things but when it comes down to it, our desires and aspirations will determine our choices and in turn affect our level of commitment.

Orpah wanted a family, a husband, a home, joy in marriage. Naomi could not give her these, but she remained out of duty. However, the moment Naomi gave her the opportunity to leave, she left in search of what she really wanted.

Ruth, on the other hand, was committed to the relationship she had built with her mother-in-law, even after her husband died. She valued their relationship and decided to stay with her because she understood the meaning of a covenant relationship. Do not just break relationships thoughtlessly or on a whim. Once one enters into a covenant relationship, one must bear in mind that they are in it for life or until the Lord decides otherwise.

Entering a covenant relationship with someone means one is deciding to follow him/her, and to attach one's destiny to them. It means one is deciding to:

1. Go with them anywhere
2. Live where they live or ask you to live
3. Relate with who they relate with or instruct you to relate with
4. Believe in what they believe in and invest your trust in them

Although we may not need to literally do every one of these things, when we look at the terms of a covenant relationship, we would see that we may only have one or two covenant relationships in life.

Promising to be with someone forever is different from entering a covenant relationship. The bond is different. A covenant relationship is a much higher level of commitment, such that one cannot separate. If they move, one moves, if they stay, one stays, one lives where they live, relates with who they relate with, believes in what they believe in, dies where they die. I do believe this is the type of commitment expected in marriage.

Notice that Ruth's covenant relationship was not made manifest until after she was widowed. It is correct that marriage is a type of covenant relationship, a physical typology of the spiritual covenant relationship we are talking about. It is not something you rush into or take lightly.

Ruth's story does not really begin until after she enters her covenant relationship. Your story will not begin until you enter your covenant relationship, because your destiny is linked to the person you attach yourself to. Literally, how you end up in life is determined by who you go into covenant with.

PUTTING OTHERS FIRST

"And they said unto her, Surely we will return with thee unto thy people..."

- Ruth 1:10

After Naomi suffered the tragic loss of her husband and two sons, she decided to return to her home country to live out the rest of her days alone in her misery. Orpah and Ruth, her two daughters-in-law and fellow widows, were both ready to return with her to Judah, but rather than accept their company in her time of depression, she tried hard to dissuade them from coming along with her.

Naomi, considerate of their youth and that they would be strangers in Israel, asked Orpah on two separate occasions to return to her home before Orpah decided to leave the old widow. Ruth, however refused to be dissuaded.

In times of loss and depression, it is very normal to want to be left alone, giving valid excuses why those around us should leave.

In our walk with The Lord, we all have those moments when we feel so low after life has dealt us a hard blow and all we want to do is shut the world out and wallow in our misery. We see here that even Naomi felt that way too.

On the flip side, we all may have had that friend or family member who seems to be pushing you away, giving you reasons to not want to be around them and making excuses for you to leave them alone. It is easy to get so caught up in our own lives and our own issues that we do not actually stop to notice that maybe, just maybe, that person is sinking into a deep despair because of the things they are going through.

Tragedy is a part of life. There is no doubt that Ruth was hurting too. She had just lost her brother-in-law and husband also. She was a widow just like Naomi, suffering and in pain, but somehow, she found the strength to put her troubles aside and be there for someone else when they needed her to be, even when they did not want it.

In our search for God, this is a key concept we must grasp; **learning to give service to others first, no matter what we are going through.** (See Matthew 20:25-28.)

Let's be real; it's not easy.

When we do, like Ruth, decide to embark on this journey to care for others, there are different things that will try to dissuade us from staying the course.

FIVE TESTS OF COMMITMENT

1. Hardships *(Mark 4: 16-17)*

When things get tough, it is easier to just abandon the whole process. It is easy to do what Orpah did and accept the excuses we are given. Remember though, no matter how good a reason is for not doing something, it is still an excuse if the thing has not been done.

Hard times will always test our commitment to a thing or a person. We know we are growing and have a solid commitment to someone when, even in our hardship, we can put them first, and they know it too.

2. Loss *(Matthew 19: 20-22, 28-29)*

When the price for a thing gets steeper, it becomes easier to walk away. This is human nature; everyone wants to thrive. Everyone is looking for greener pastures, something better than what they have, without having to pay too high a price for it.

We trade things of value for things we value even more than them. When we give up something of high value to us for something we perceive is of a lesser value, we feel we have incurred a loss.

The presence or anticipation of loss has the power to turn anyone away from their decision to be there for others. We think, "It will cost me too much to help you." And so we say to them, "God bless you... I'm praying for you... it is well... this too, shall pass" instead of actually doing something to improve the persons situation.

The rich man who came to see Jesus left because his value of his wealth was so great to him that it would have cost him too much to follow Jesus. So also, a lot of people are turned away from this path when they face the reality of sacrificing or losing things they esteem highly or hold very dear.

It will cost us something to be there for others, to put our needs aside, believing that God will take care of us as we focus on helping others.

It is a hard thing to do and so, we must also be aware that people are naturally ungrateful. They are forgetful and they are equalizers. When we help someone, we must not expect them to be grateful or even remember what we have done for them. Most people rather repay kindness with hurtful and sometimes unkind behaviour towards those who have helped them.

Be aware of this and guard your heart. People are ungrateful and forgetful.

3. Time *(Deuteronomy 8: 11-14)*

Time is a great determinant of one's steadfastness. Because someone has decided to do something today does not guarantee that they will always be doing it.

A lot of things change with time, and it gets easier to change one's mind or to forget after a while. We need to be aware of this and not let the passage of time weaken our resolve.

There is a law of degeneration that works on everything with time. As time goes by, the law of degeneration or diminishing returns takes effect and things start to weaken in quality. This is also the case with our resolve to seek God.

Loyalty today does not necessarily mean loyalty tomorrow.

4. Others *(2 Corinthians 6: 17)*

It is easy to follow the crowd. It is easy to be persuaded by other people's actions to leave one's own journey. It is easy to say, "everyone is doing this, so I'll do the same." But the thing is, Ruth chose the difficult path, she chose to do something different from what her sister-in-law was doing, something different from what her family and her people were doing.

Ruth decided to be different and stuck to that decision despite what others were doing.

The call to God is a call to come out from among our friends and family, to be separate.

5. Distance *(Job 19:13)*

Another great test of one's commitment to a person or thing is distance. When there is distance, communication can sometimes wane and this in turn leads to a break down in the relationship.

The world is becoming smaller with the aid of technology but that does not mean distance does not take its toll on one's commitment.

Realise that distance does influence things and actively move to counteract these effects.

LAYING A GOOD FOUNDATION

"So they two went until they came to Bethlehem. And it came to pass, when they were come to Bethlehem..."

- Ruth 1:19

1. Accept that your own story never starts with you

Your background is always a part of someone else's story, and you cannot change that.

Here, we see that the sisters-in-law made two different decisions that were not about or only affecting them. Orpah returned to her people and her gods while Ruth returned to Naomi's people and Naomi's God.

This is why one's background is important, because no matter where we go, we carry our learned experiences with us, and it can be very easy in hard times to fall back on our background knowledge and beliefs.

It is easy to return to what is familiar.

You see, when Jesus died, some of his disciples returned to fishing, because that was what they knew and were used to.

> "Simon Peter saith unto them, "I go a fishing." They say unto him, "We also go with thee.' They went forth and entered into a ship immediately and that night they caught nothing."
>
> - John 21: 3

In understanding this, we can see that the disciples' backgrounds were not shaped by themselves but laid out by their parents and others for them to follow (e.g., James and John, the sons of Zebedee, whose father was a fisherman and laid the foundation for them to become fishermen too).

The sooner we understand this principle, the easier it becomes for us to move forward; our stories are built upon the lives of others, they did not start, neither do they end, with us. Once we have understood and accepted this, we can then look into our lives and see the things that have shaped them and led us to where we are, as well as what we can do to influence ourselves in order to get to where we want to be.

2. Keep the right company

> "Do not be fooled by those who say such things, for "bad company corrupts good character." Think carefully about what is right and stop sinning. For to your shame I say that some of you do not know God at all."
>
> - 1 Corinthians 15: 33-34 (New Living Translation)

When we associate with people (join ourselves to them), we do not just join ourselves to them, we join ourselves to the things they stand for and believe in. For example, in the case of King Solomon, joining himself to foreign women meant joining himself to their gods.

When we decide to join ourselves to someone, we must make sure we know who or what a person's God/gods (beliefs and core principles) are before we do so. We have to make sure we know the person's background because, as mentioned, that person is also building on the foundation laid by those gone before them.

Once you have a good understanding of where you are and where you need to be, allow the Lord to direct you to the right people and situations that can influence your course and help lay a new foundation for your future to be built upon.

3. Lay a good foundation for those to come

> *"For He established a testimony in Jacob, and appointed a law in Israel, which He commanded our fathers, that they should make them known to their children. That the generation to come might know them..."*
>
> *- Psalm 78: 5-7*

Since we have established the fact that one's story does not start with them, we need to understand that we are also laying the foundations for other people's stories to begin.

What kind of foundation will you lay?

In the time of trouble, Orpah returned to what she knew and believed while Ruth was bold enough to accept a new way, carve out a new path in faith, and follow God to build a better foundation for her future and her descendants.

It is true that your background taught you the tools that have brought you this far, but if you realize that there are things in your background that need to be changed, or things you need to do now to shape a culture of seeking the Lord's presence in your life and the lives of your children, make the change now. Nobody should be able to dissuade you from what God has spoken to you about, no matter how hopeless the situation may look.

DEALING WITH THE PAST

"And she said unto them, call me Mara: for the Almighty hath dealt very bitterly with me."

- Ruth 1:20

In Ruth 1: 19-22, Naomi and Ruth arrive home and the first thing that happens, people start to talk.

Some external conversations that go on may affect us, but our internal dialogue can destroy or create us. In addition, our past experiences largely affect the things we say to and about ourselves.

Naomi's dialogue, at her return to Bethlehem, shows that her perception of her identity had been changed by her past experiences, to the point where she changes her name to reflect her past circumstances.

Sometimes, we allow what we have been through to affect who we are, forgetting that what that is now behind us. We can sometimes find ourselves trapped in a place and time that no longer exists in the present. Naomi was home, she had her daughter in law who was later described as being better than seven sons, yet she could not see what she had because she was so blinded by what she had lost.

> "And he shall be unto thee a restorer of thy life, and a nourisher of thine old age: for thy daughter in law, which loveth thee, which is better to thee than seven sons, hath born him"
>
> - Ruth 4:15

1. Understand you have nothing to prove to anyone

It is true that people will always talk; they will have some-thing to say about other people's situations. Whether we decide to entertain them or not is our choice.

It is true that life can be hard and, if we are a little mature, we will understand that we will have to overcome a lot of challenges in life, but how we allow these experiences affect what we say, think and feel about ourselves is very important.

Our internal conversations are reflected in our conversations with others and many times, especially when we have been in a low place, it makes us feel better talking about it.

A lot of people want to share the things they have been through, not necessarily because they want help or they want to deal with the issues, but because the pain of sometimes retelling previous sufferings can become addictive.

Yes, it is possible to become addicted to pain and self-pity and make excuses for where we are and how our lives have turned out, but the truth is, we do not have to prove anything to anyone except ourselves and our God.

Like Naomi, we may have gone out full and returned empty, but that is really nobody's business. Not everyone needs to know everything that is going on in our lives.

Because people are listening, that does not mean that they care or are going to do anything about it. We do not need to try to convince people that we have had it rough or gain their sympathy. Rather, what we need is to dispel the evil thoughts and spirits of depression and fear that keep us trapped in the same place.

If you are ready to get help, speak to someone you can trust to give you spirit-filled guidance, advice or support. Speak to someone, not because you want to talk about how justified you are in feeling the way you do, but because you genuinely want help to move on from your past and advance in your walk with God.

2. Understand you are not your past experiences

Another thing Naomi did when she got back was allow her past to dictate or affect who she was. She changed her name, her identity, who she was, because of what she had been through, even though the Bible tells us she came into Judah at a good time, at the beginning of harvest.

Like Naomi, we acknowledge the hand of God in our affairs, both good and bad. This does not mean that we let these experiences define us. When we have been through a lot of hardship, it is sometimes hard to realize when it has come to an end and the storm clouds have begun to scatter.

Often, it is easy to gain our identities from what we have been or are going through. However, we must note that when we gain our identities from our past experiences, we cripple ourselves for the future.

3. Understand that your story is bigger than you

This is the beginning of Ruth's story at a difficult time in the life of Naomi, just as Elisha's story began at a difficult time in the life of Elijah as well as David's story, at a difficult time in the life of Saul.

Many times, our stories begin at a difficult time in the life of someone else, and vice versa. This is again why we need to learn to put other people's needs above ours. We may never know who laid the foundation for our stories to begin, or whose story's foundation we are laying.

God will bring us to significant places at significant times because He has a timeline for everything. It is not by coincidence that we meet the people we do when we do. It is not by coincidence that you are reading this book right now.

As we walk with God and trust in Him, we mustn't let our experiences define us, but rather allow Him to use them to help others and also use that as a springboard to manifest His Glory in our lives.

Sometimes the things we go through are in preparation for the people coming after us.

THE KEY TO RELATIONSHIPS

"And the second is like, namely this, Thou shalt love thy neighbour as thyself. There is none other commandment greater than these."

- Mark 12:31

One major key to success in life is the way we relate with others. This is also true in our walk with God.

Our rise or fall depends on our relationships; how far we will go and what we will be able to achieve in life is mainly dependent on our relationships.

To fully grasp the key to *relationships*, we must understand these principles:

1. There are different types of relationships you can have with various people
2. Different types of relationships yield different types of fruits
3. Your success or failure hinges on your relationships

Some relationships are more valuable than others and identifying which is which will be crucial to our success. There are certain people that God has brought, and will bring, into our lives to help us fulfil our life's purposes. These people are destiny changers; they are the fathers, pastors, mentors, teachers, sons, daughters, friends, brethren, associates, mentees.

Learn to identify these destiny changers and do all that is within your power to preserve your relationship with them.

BUILDING A RELATIONSHIP WITH GOD

Our relationships with others reflect our relationship with God. How we relate to the people around us serves as a reflection of how our relationship with God is.

We can also use them to develop our relationship with God. If we can love those we can see, then we are more likely to love those we cannot see. We can practise and develop our relationship with God through the way we relate to the people around us.

There are three basic relationships:

1. Relationships with those above you

These are the leaders and authority figures in our lives. They have been chosen by God and we are meant to relate with them as unto God. If we want to check how we relate with God, we can check how we relate with the authority figures in our lives.

Do we listen to them? Do we honour them? Do we respect them? Do we love them? Do we pray for them? Do we trust them?

We must identify the different types of authority in our lives and the hierarchy of these authorities. We must recognize the delegated authority in our lives. Sometimes, the person(s) may not have a position or a title but by virtue of the relationship they have or the things they do and/or the person's work in our lives, they are actually an authority figure that has been delegated to us.

2. Relationships with those beside you

These are the people that we would see as on our level. Our co-equals, if I should put it that way. These includes our comrades, team, etc. and we need to respect them.

Learn from God. The way the Godhead relates with each other is the way we should relate with them. With one mind and spirit, it is essential to know and understand everyone's strengths and weaknesses while working with them.

Although God can do everything, it is not everything that He does. The same goes with Jesus and the Holy Spirit. We see that, although they have the power to do so, they do not work independent of one another.

There are three sub-divisions of this type of relationship:

Level One

This is the relationship the Father had with the Son and the Spirit. He's the first person in the Godhead so He's basically the leader, but at the same time, you see that there are things that He will not interfere with because they have been given to the Son or the Spirit to deal with.

Once Jesus or the Spirit says so, it is sealed even though He is God and He has the power to do what He wants.

This is the best kind of team leader ever; one that respects and believes in their team and will back them up all the way.

Level Two

This is the relationship the son has with the Father. Although he can do what he wants, he has absolute trust in what the Father says and does not do things without the Father's knowledge and consent. This may be the reason why the Father has such total confidence in the Son.

The Father trusts the son because the son trusts the Father absolutely, no secrets, no hiding, no fear, no shame. This is the relationship that a wife should have with her husband. This is the kind of relationship that an assistant should have with their leader or their head. This is what keeps a team together.

Level Three

The relationship of the Spirit. It takes wisdom in a leader to know that his power lies in his people and his relationship with the people is what determines how he can control the power.

The Holy Spirit is the power of God. He has been delegated all the power and is the driving force behind the work. Whatever God wants to move, He moves through the Spirit, He creates through the Spirit. This is the relationship the normal team members have with the leader.

A team is a unit and in fact, a team cannot be great if all its members do not play their part properly. Sometimes, we may have to be the powerhouse of our coequals, getting things done, being the brawn while someone else is the brain. It does not mean that we are less than them or not on their level, it just means that we have a different function in the team at that point in time, and in actual fact, the team would not be able to work without either of us.

It is not the case that we are meant to switch off our brains and just act on instruction, it just means that we must have enough faith in our team to trust the decisions of our comrades.

The Holy Ghost is the wisdom of God but does not question God, He does what God says because they are that in sync. This type of unity is the kind of relationship God expects us to have with our comrades, our brethren in Christ.

Because these levels are not fixed, you need to identify which level you fit in with your comrades at any given time and flow accordingly.

3. Relationships with those below you in hierarchy

How we treat the people below us should reflect how God treats us. We are *meant* to treat them the way God treats us. we are meant to reflect God to them. We are meant to be the image of God to them. This is what it means to be 'Christlike' as it is being like Christ to others. It is the ability of others to see Christ in or through us.

RELATIONSHIP INGREDIENTS

The following are a few of the main keys needed in building relationships:

1. Honesty and transparency

For the relationship to work, honesty must be present. We should learn to be completely open and transparent. We must let ourselves be seen as we really are. We must not fear rejection or judgement. You are who you are, and you need to accept yourself, so that others can accept you while working with you.

Strong and lasting relationships are founded upon honesty. Honesty of self, of one's opinions, of one's decisions. You cannot live in the shadows and expect to gain someone's trust.

We should give of ourselves wholly and not hold back.

2. Trust

Having total confidence in the people we are building relationships with is important. We should believe the best of them and, as long as it is founded on the Word of God, respect their decisions and believe they have/had good reasons for their choices, even though these choices may not necessarily be what we would have gone for.

3. Humility

Humility is knowing who we are in relation to God and to those around us. The opposite of humility is pride.

Pride is seen in one's estimation of themselves, whether high or low. Thinking that we are greater than we are or thinking more highly of ourselves than we ought to, is the manifestation of pride that is most identified by people. This is mostly because when someone elevates themselves above us, our own pride takes a hit and so it is easier for us to notice it.

The second, which is more subtle than the high estimation of oneself is a low estimation of oneself, or what we call low self-esteem. This is a form of pride because it is putting our evaluation of ourselves over what God says we are and who we really are in relation to others.

We ought to identify who we are and where we are at in relation to God and others. We should have an accurate assessment of ourselves, our strengths, and weaknesses. We mustn't think we are greater or less than we are. We need to learn to have an accurate assessment of ourselves and those around us as well. And we must not be judgemental about this.

If some people can do certain things better than us, there is no shame in letting them do it. That is how a team grows and the Church of God gets stronger. It does not change who we are as individuals or what we are worth to God.

If you notice, true relationships are deep. Simply put, you cannot be close to everyone. **You need to be selective of the people you get close to.**

Notice that, although God loves everyone and wants everyone to be reconciled back to Himself, He does not open Himself and His heart to everyone. He is very selective of those people He lets in. He is very mindful of those He chooses to come close to Him, and these three ingredients are part of the main criteria for His choices.

He chooses people who are completely honest and transparent with Him, He chooses people who trust Him and have complete faith in Him and He chooses people who are humble, who know believe in and trust Him.

Though we are all co-equals, we are not all the same. It is necessary to know and respect this in order to develop healthy and lasting relationships.

WHAT IT MEANS TO BE A FRIEND OF JESUS.

"Ye have not chosen me, but I have chosen you, and ordained you, that ye should go and bring forth fruit, and that your fruit should remain: that whatsoever ye shall ask of the Father in my name, he may give it you."

- John 15:16

The love of Jesus is not conditional, but his friendship is.

Before Jesus was crucified, he told his disciples several things about God, Heaven, and himself (see John 15:12-15). One of the things he told them was that he no longer related to them as a master would to his servants. Somewhere along the line, his relationship with them changed and he then related with them as his friends.

Jesus said that the difference between a friend and a servant is the level of revelation one has.

When we have a real friend, we tell them our secrets, we do not hide things from them. The greatest sign that Jesus is my friend is that he tells me things.

When Jesus tells me things, I get a chance to prove to him whether I am his friend or not. You see, it is possible to see someone as a friend even though they do not see you the same way.

I remember once, a person I related with was saying a lot of negative things about me, accusing me of things I had not done and speaking ill of me. I got to find out about this and was quite upset because in all of this, they had not once hinted to me that there was a problem. I, following my pastor's advice, chose to say nothing about it.

About a week after they had acted out, I received a series of messages from them, including one in which they mentioned how they thought we were just two friends who had forgotten how to care about each other properly.

I remember thinking as I read the message, "Who told you we were friends?" And in that moment, I realised what the problem was; I saw them differently to the way they saw me, and this made them upset because they felt I was not treating them as a friend should.

Assessing the situation, I retreated and searched my heart for why I did not see this person as a friend; after all, I had been taught by my pastor to build genuine friendships with the people around me. What was different about this person that made me not see them as a friend? In assessing my heart, I found the answer: I could not trust them.

I realised I did not want them as my friend because I could not trust them, and this was because of previous series of situations where I had advised them, and they had chosen to act contrary to my advice. Once, they even said to me, "I hear all you say, but I'm going to do what I want."

These series of events brought me to the conclusion that this person did not take my advice because they inherently did not agree with me, believe in me or the things I believed in and so did otherwise, and for this reason, I made the decision to keep them at arm's length.

They saw me as a friend, but I did not see them the same way.

Now, we sing songs and tell people how we are "a friend of God," however when we get down to it, does Jesus really see us as friends? Jesus told us the requirement for being his friend; simply doing what he says. That is how he knows he can trust us and reveal His secrets to us.

Could it be possible that you see Jesus as your friend and yet, he does not see you the same way?

ABRAHAM, A FRIEND OF GOD

"But thou, Israel, art my servant, Jacob whom I have chosen, the seed of Abraham my friend."

- Isaiah 41:8

The scriptures tell us about Abraham being a friend of God. For a long time, I wondered why God would call Abraham His friend, of all the people in the world He had to choose from. In the following scripture, God shows us why He made that choice.

In Genesis 18:17-19, God deliberates whether to treat Abraham as His friend and tell him His plans. God settles on telling Abraham and He explains why He has come to this decision; He says in verse 18, in simple words, that Abraham can be trusted to do whatever The Lord commands him.

Abraham could be trusted to obey God's word and even lead his whole household to do the same, so God was prepared to reveal to him the secret plans He wanted to carry out.

Just as Jesus told his disciples, we see here that God's choice of a friend is someone who can be trusted to do what He commands or instructs.

There is no formula for God. I will not be so presumptuous as to assume that we can "crack the code" or devise a formula for becoming a friend of God. God is all sovereign and almighty and has the right to decide who He wants to draw close to Himself.

Jesus told his disciples plainly that they did not choose him, rather he chose them. After explaining to them that he loves them with the greatest love ever and he sees them as friends, after telling them that his real friends are those whom he can trust to do what he says, he further made it clear that it was not by their choice, but by his that they even had the opportunity to be his friend.

What I want you to understand is this**: if we have been given the opportunity to do so, Jesus shows we can prove ourselves to be real friends by our obedience to his commandments.** As to whether we will be chosen or favoured with the opportunity, that still remains his ultimate choice, so let us use the opportunities we get wisely.

FAITH AND BELIEF

> *"Abraham believed God, and it was imputed unto him for righteousness: and he was called the Friend of God. Ye see then how that by works a man is justified, and not by faith only."*
>
> *- James 2:23-24*

Abraham was called the friend of God because he believed God. If we relate belief to the wind, we have a good analogy to understand faith.

SELLING INTERNATIONAL AIR

A friend of mine came to visit one day. He told me of how he planned to travel to America to specialize in his field and then head to Nigeria to run his father's company. He laughed about how his friend in Nigeria had chided him for wanting to leave America, telling him, "I just want to be able to smell the air there."

We went on to talk about business ideas around importing and exporting air from different countries, compressing it into aerosol canisters so people could spray and smell the air from different places, no matter where they were. As much as it would be a great business venture, it sounds ridiculous because all we would essentially be doing is selling empty canisters. You see, although the bottles will be full of air, air is something you cannot see.

★★★

We cannot see the wind, but we can tell it is there by its effects. Staring outside my bedroom window, I am watching the leaves and branches dance outside and from this I can tell it is a windy day, but I cannot see any wind like lines or swirls used to depict it in cartoons and animated images. I simply cannot see wind!

I can confidently say, "Look! Can you not see it is very windy?" And whoever I am speaking to will be able to see it is windy by the leaves swaying in the trees and by the whistling of the wind as it passes quickly through narrow spaces, but they cannot see the wind. What they are looking at are the effects the wind is having on the things around it.

They can see what is happening due to the presence of the wind.

It is similar with faith. You and I cannot physically see faith, but we can tell that it is there, by the things happening due to its presence. We can tell what a person believes in by the things that happen due to the presence of that belief.

If I believe that it will rain, as I go out, I will take an umbrella or raincoat, or even might decide to stay indoors. These actions, or any others I take in response to my belief that it will rain is what you can use to tell I believe it will rain. These actions are the works that justify my faith.

The scripture says that faith is the evidence of the things not seen.

> *"Now faith is the substance of things hoped for, the evidence of things not seen."*
>
> - Hebrews 11:1

It is what proves the existence of something we cannot see. Like the leaves moving in the wind, faith is the actions you take because of an invisible present belief. Faith is not the invisible presence itself; it is the evidence of the presence.

Faith is the proof of what you believe.

It is the actions resulting from the things we say we believe, which is why faith without works is dead. (See James 2:17-24.)

Just as wind is air in motion, we can conclude that faith is belief in action.

FAITH AND THE KNOWLEDGE OF GOD

"And Jesus answering saith unto them, Have faith in God..."

- Mark 11:22

Jesus gave us an instruction; have faith in God. He then went on further to explain how by teaching that, if we believe in our hearts that it would, what we say will come to pass. In other words, we can create the things we believe are possible by simply speaking them. If we believe the mountain can be moved, speak to it to move and it will, but do not speak if we do not believe or we would not get that result. Actions fuelled by belief can make the impossible possible.

Here are two things we can learn from this:

1. Belief without actions yield no results

That we believe it is possible for the impossible to happen, does not automatically mean it will come to pass.

A lot of Christians say we believe in a lot of things and, no doubt, these things are true. However, many of us do not go beyond that point, we do not act on what we say we believe and thus do not get the results.

2. Actions without belief yield no results

It is easy to follow someone else's faith-filled actions and then get disappointed because we do not get the same results they did. The reason for this is that we believed the results they had were due to the actions we saw the person carry out alone, and not in relation to what the person actually believed in that led them to carry out those actions.

We take action without belief and end up with no results.

From all of this, we can summarize Jesus's lesson to the disciples on faith as this:

Have faith in God. Believing without acting will not yield results, so also acting without believing will result in nothing. Faith is acting on what you believe in your heart, therefore act on the belief you have in God, and you will be able to do the impossible.

When you act on what you believe about God, you will see great results.

The beliefs we hold in our hearts about the character and nature of God are very important. This is so because our trust in someone's words stem from our trust in their character. If we do not trust a person's character, it is hard to believe that they are telling us the truth.

If we believe someone to be a pathological liar, it is highly unlikely that we will believe what they tell us without first confirming from other more reliable sources. So, it is also with our relationship with

God; if we do not know and are not fully convinced of His character and heart, we will find it very difficult to believe the things He tells us without having concrete physical evidence.

This teaching on Jesus's lesson of faith in God would not be accurate without explaining that the disciples had been with Jesus for some time now and he had taught them many things about the nature and commandments of God. Hence, telling them to act on the things they believe about God is in reference to all the things he had already taught them about God.

If we do not know God or anything about him, how do we act on something we have not even believed in yet? This was the same question Paul posed to the Romans:

"How then shall they call on him in whom they have not believed? and how shall they believe in him of whom they have not heard? and how shall they hear without a preacher?"

- Romans 10:14

How can we have faith in someone we have not believed in? And how can we believe in someone we have not heard about? And how can we hear if someone has not come to tell us?

From the questions above, it shows it would have been an unreasonable instruction for Jesus to tell the disciples to have faith in God if he had not already preached to them and they did not already believe. Jesus had already taught his disciples about God before he got to this point. So also, for us to get to the point where we can "have faith in God," we must also have learned something about the nature of God.

SEVEN THINGS TO KNOW ABOUT GOD

1. God has a will *(Mark 3:31-35)*
Jesus taught his disciples that God had a will. God has His likes and dislikes as well as desires and plans He wishes to be carried out, which is the criteria for inclusion into His family; obeying His will.

2. God has a kingdom *(Mark 4:10-11)*
Jesus taught His disciples in private that God had a kingdom and his teachings were secrets of the kingdom.

3. God has secrets *(Mark 4:11-12)*
Jesus taught the disciples that mysteries of God's kingdom were not things that everyone was privy to because the secrets of God, just like any secret, influence and have effects on those who hear them. God is very specific about who He reveals things to.

4. God's Kingdom is mysterious to those without but revealed to those within *(Mark 4:11)*
A clear sign that we are now in the kingdom of God is that certain things which were once mysteries to us about God and His kingdom

begin to be revealed. We begin to see and hear the things as they are, our hearts are opened, and we begin to believe things other people cannot understand.

Jesus taught that God's mysteries revealed had an effect, as they brought about a change in those who heard and believed them. They were not revealed to people whose hearts were hard as His words would have no effect on them.

Would a great business tycoon tell us his secret to his empire if he knew we would not believe him or use the information he provided us with? Why do we expect God to tell everyone His secrets when they would not believe Him or use the knowledge well?

5. God is a God that does great things *(Mark 5:19)*

Although Jesus was instructing the man who was delivered from demons which caused madness in him, a lesson to be learnt here about God—and I'm sure the disciples learnt this too—is that God does great things.

6. God is compassionate *(Mark 5:19)*

Another important lesson to learn here is that God has compassion. It was a popular belief back then, and even now, that God is a merciless God who punished all wrong by sickness, suffering and eventually burning in hell.

The preconceptions are understandable; however, they are

inaccurate.

Yes, sin can bring about sickness, suffering, death, and eternal damnation. However, it has a price on its own and God should not be held responsible for the consequences of one's actions.

God is a just God and it is wisdom to fear Him. However, we must not forget that He is a loving and compassionate God who freely gives us everything, including His only son, to save us from the destruction we as humans so eagerly run to.

7. God has a commandment *(Mark 7:6-8)*

A commandment is a law. It is a prescribed rule in accordance with which things are done. God has a universal rule which some like to refer to as the *Golden Rule*.

★★★

> *"This is my commandment, That ye love one another, as I have loved you."*
>
> *- John 15:12*

God's law is the law of love, and it is the law He operates by. God wants us to love and to do everything in and motivated by love. This is the guiding principle God runs His kingdom by, and anything other than love is going against the law.

Anything done that is not in accordance with the law of love is a crime and a sin according to God.

> *"Whosoever committeth sin transgresseth also the law: for sin is the transgression of the law."*
>
> *- 1 John 3:4*

FAITH AND HEARING

"And he said unto them, take heed what ye hear: with what measure ye mete, it shall be measured to you: and unto you that hear shall more be given."

- Mark 4:24

If faith is acting on what we believe, then what we believe becomes very important. We believe the things we see and hear from sources we assume are established and reliable, like research findings and people we trust. Therefore, what we see and hear becomes very crucial in the forming and establishing of our faith in God.

What we hear affects us, whether we like it or not.

Jesus warns us to be careful of and attentive to the things we hear. As he mentioned to his disciples, he spoke in parables to the people because the secrets of the kingdom were not for them to know, and this would then explain why his proceeding statement seemed somewhat like a parable; "with what measure ye mete, it shall be measured to you: and unto you that hear shall more be given."

If we take the liberty of deciphering this proverb in the light of our teaching on faith, and in its context of Jesus's teaching in the chapter on the *Kingdom and the Word of God*, we would see that Jesus explains to his disciples that the kingdom of God operates in a very similar manner to that of farming: a seed is planted and, depending on what kind of soil it is planted in, it either grows and bears fruit or it does not.

In other words, we hear what God says and, depending on the state of our hearts, His Word either grows to elicit an action which produces great results, or it does not.

Jesus then goes on to explain that no one lights a candle just so they can hide the light, but rather places the light somewhere visible to make a difference to their surroundings. So also, the things that we believe in our hearts cannot be hidden. They will eventually affect the way we speak and the things we do, they will produce fruit in a way that is obvious for all to see.

It is at this point that Jesus then admonishes us (his disciples) to be mindful of the things we hear, going on to explain in a proverbial manner that how much we believe in the Word of God (with what measure ye mete) will determine the results of our faith (it shall be measured to you).

In summary, he explains that the more you believe, the greater the effect (and unto you that hear, shall more be given).

By this, we understand that to have faith in God's Word, what we hear must be of the utmost importance to us. If we kept hearing that eating spicy chicken wings caused cancer (I am not saying that this is true), and studies were published online about correlations between spicy chicken wings consumers and cancer patients, and afterwards, we saw that shops stopped selling spicy chicken wings, sooner or later, we would begin to believe this was true.

THE PLASTIC LETTUCE.

While I was studying at university, a friend of mine and I often visited a local Oriental restaurant that served a buffet to students at a discounted price. We introduced many friends to this all-you-can-eat restaurant and even celebrated our birthdays there because they would give the celebrant a special cake.

I often wondered though, after observing the large proportions of food consumed by myself and my friends, how this restaurant ever made a profit. Surely, we were consuming more food than what we paid could afford, even if we paid the full price.

One day, someone I know mentioned how these restaurants were serving plastic food. I shrugged off these absurd and erroneous accusations as conspiracy theories. After all, I am sure I would notice if I were eating plastic. It was not until I came across a video online that I started to take these accusations seriously.

In the video, a manufacturing plant in China was producing real looking plastic Lettuce!

Following on from my watching the video, a very prominent all-you-can-eat Oriental restaurant was suddenly closed. I remember walking past the building and saying to myself, "they must have been selling plastic food, that's why."

Now I think back on it, the restaurant was closed down due to health and safety issues with the building and the video I watched could very easily have been a toy company or a company producing plastic fruit and vegetables for aesthetic or advertisement purposes but, because of what I had heard, I started to believe the food served in such places did indeed contain plastic and, eventually, I stopped visiting the establishment.

Understand this; what you hear will affect you in some way or another, whether you choose to believe me or not.

When we see and hear certain things frequently and from sources that we tend to believe are credible, we begin to believe what we have heard sooner or later.

If we keep hearing that God is someone who delights in punishing people, we would explain things we think have gone wrong as probably being a punishment from God, and eventually begin to believe every negative event to be God's punishment for something or the other.

FAITH AND OBEDIENCE

"By faith Abraham, when he was called to go out into a place which he should after receive for an inheritance, obeyed; and he went out, not knowing whither he went."

- Hebrews 11:8

I assume, by this point, we have understood that when we believe in something strongly enough, it affects us in ways that make it obvious to others what we believe.

When we genuinely believe in something, we cannot but act upon it, and this action, based upon what we believe, is what we call faith, the evidence of our unseen belief.

If we genuinely believe in the Word of God, we will act upon it. This action in obedience to the Word of God is our faith. We can therefore conclude with confidence that faith is obedience to the Word of God, and obedience to the Word of God is faith.

Abraham, the one God called friend, obeyed the instruction of God to go where God wanted him to. He obeyed the instruction because he believed in the promise God made to him to give him an inheritance. He trusted that God was able to fulfil the promise, and that He would, and he acted upon this belief by obeying the instruction to go.

The more we come to know about God, read His Word, discover His likes and dislikes as well as His dos and don'ts, we begin to receive counsel and guidance from Him as He begins to instruct us, with our closeness to Him being determined by our obedience to His statutes.

> *"Jesus answered and said unto him, if a man love me, he will keep my words: and my Father will love him, and we will come unto him, and make our abode with him."*
>
> *- John 14:23*

Many of us believe what people say, but God looks at our hearts and measures by our actions. God's test of love is spelled out in the verse above "if any man loves me, he will keep my words."

Obedience to God's word is a clear sign that we love Him, and that draws His presence to us, draws Him closer to us. The more we obey, the closer we get.

In our quest to become friends of God, one great lesson we can learn is that faith is an integral key to closeness with God.

> *"But without faith it is impossible to please him: for he that cometh to God must believe that he is, and that he is a rewarder of them that diligently seek him."*
>
> *- Hebrews 11:6*

THREE KEY CONCEPTS OF FAITH

1. Faith in God is an instruction, not a suggestion

> *"And Jesus answering saith unto them, have faith in God."*
>
> *- Mark 11:22*

Jesus instructs his disciples to have faith in God. The substance of the things we hope for should be in God, the evidence of the things we cannot see should be in God. To walk, live in and manifest the Kingdom of God, the things we believe and act upon should be what God has said. Our faith must be in God. This is an instruction, not a suggestion.

2. What you believe is revealed by the things you say

> *"... for of the abundance of the heart his mouth speaketh."*
>
> *- Luke 6:45*

It is particularly important to understand that the things we believe in our hearts are the things we will say. Our beliefs are not things we can see physically but its effects will tell us that they are there often by what we say.

Sometimes we may not even realise what is in our hearts until we are provoked into speaking certain words.

Now, some people may argue that anything said in the heat of the moment or when one is provoked, should not be held as valid, but if I squeeze a lemon, the only thing I expect from it is lemon juice, no matter how hard I squeeze. This is because only what is in it can come out of it.

So, if in the heat of the moment, or when the pressure is applied, certain words proceed from your mouth, you may not like to accept it but, take it from me, that thing is somewhere in your heart.

THE PRESSURE OF CORRECTION

I visited a dear friend of mine (still a dear friend) and during my visit, they said to me, "If there is anything you see that I am doing wrong, please correct me so I can get better."

I thought to myself, this is a very mature young person who is actively looking to be corrected and sharpened, so I decided to test them.

I said to them, "Oh, but I do not see why you would want me to correct you."

And to that they responded, "No, I really want you to tell me if you think I'm going the wrong way."

So, with that, believing they were serious, I explained to them how, sometimes we say things in a manner that comes across to others as rude or disrespectful. I suggested to them to maybe consider how the recipient may understand and interpret their words before they make certain statements, especially if they are speaking to someone older than them.

To my surprise, this person suddenly became agitated and defensive, arguing with me about people misunderstanding them. I agreed and suggested that maybe the reason for the misunderstanding was the way they phrased certain things.

This person's argument degenerated to shouts, to the point that I apologised for correcting them and even called a mediator to help explain that I was only suggesting to them, as per their request, something they might want to work on.

Eventually, this person shouted in their anger, "... it is because you are rude and proud!"

I was shocked to hear that someone who was like a daughter and little sister to me, that someone who often told me how much they loved me and grateful they were to have me in their lives, would say to me that I am rude and proud.

Unknown to them, although they often behaved as though they loved me and believed in me, and even promoted my books, in their heart, what they believed about me was that I was rude and proud.

After that statement, a lot of things that had happened in the past began to make perfect sense.

A lot of actions I had put off as childishness and ignorance began to explain themselves. This person believed in their heart that I was rude and proud, and it affected the way they behaved but, because it was not something obvious to either of us, we did not realise that this was the person's belief about me until the pressure of correction was applied.

What is in our hearts will come out when we are under pressure, so we need to watch what we think and say in our unguarded moments, as they will tell what is in our hearts.

3. Where your faith lies is revealed by where you turn for solutions

"But when I am afraid, I will put my trust in you."

-Psalm 56:3 (New Living Translation)

Who we turn to in our time of need shows what we put our faith in. It shows who we believe has the power to make a change in our situations or to solve our problems.

Who we turn to when we need answers reveals a lot about where our faith lies. Some turn to leaders, books and blogs, others turn to search engines and celebrities.

When my phone battery began to act up, I had three options of where to get it fixed or changed. Two of those were regular corner stores and one was the phone manufacturer's store. The other stores would have got it fixed at a cheaper rate, but I chose to go to the manufacturer's store to fix it because I believed they would do the best job.

As children, we tend to run to our parents whenever we need

anything, from money to cellophane tape, because we believe that they can supply every need we come to them with. I think back on the impossible things I asked my parents for, believing that they could provide them for me. I had perfect faith that they could bring my desires to fruition.

It is the same when we deal with God. When we turn to God with our desire, it shows our faith in His ability to provide.

FAITH AND SPEAKING

> *"... for out of the abundance of the heart the mouth speaketh."*
>
> *- Matthew 12:34*

The things we say reflect what we believe in our hearts. We speak what we believe and when we speak in belief, we begin to create. Therefore, in Mark 11:22-24, Jesus taught is disciples that they would have whatever they say.

1. Speak to the situation and not just about it

> *"... For verily I say unto you, that whosoever shall say unto this mountain..."*

Jesus said whoever says to the mountain that is in their path, "Move," those are the people who see results.

Many spend their time speaking about (rather than to) the situation they are in, although it has little to no effect, which is not the principle Jesus taught. We would get faster results if we spent more time speaking to the actual situation to change instead of speaking about how we want it to or believe it is changing.

Do not neglect speaking positively about situations, because this does make a difference. It also helps our faith stay strong. However, the real change comes when we speak to the situation itself.

2. Deal with your doubt

> *"... and shall not doubt in his heart..."*

It is true that speaking what we want to see can be taken as a sign of our faith, but if we speak just because it is what we are meant to do without actually believing in what we are saying, we are unlikely to see the results.

Doubting in the heart is different from struggling in the mind. The more one struggles with a thing in their mind, the more likely it is for that doubt to take root in their heart.

Dealing with the root of our doubts is very important. Is it that we do not believe God is able? Or that He is willing to do it for us? Is it that we doubt that our words will make a difference? Or does the situation seem impossible?

Whatever it is that plants doubt in our hearts must be uprooted for us to see results.

3. Believe in the power of your words

> *"... believe that those things which he saith shall come to pass..."*

Believe that what we are saying will come to pass and believe that because we are saying it with faith, it will come to pass.

Believe your words and in the power of your words.

The same breath of God that framed the world by His words flows through us as children of God and therefore, when we speak, we should expect to have the same result.

WHILE WE WAIT

"Now there was a wealthy and influential man in Bethlehem named Boaz, who was a relative of Naomi's husband, Elimelech."

- Ruth 2:1 (New Living Translation)

In our search for God, we enter what is called a waiting period. This is a period where nothing seems to be happening. It can seem like we are stuck and almost like God has forgotten us. In these seasons, we are being given the time to develop key skills and build our character.

While we wait and develop ourselves, we need to understand a few principles to get us through as we spend our time seeking friendship with God.

1. The Principle of Vision

"Where there is no vision, the people perish: but he that keepeth the law, happy is he."

- Proverbs 29:18

Imagine sitting at the train station and just waiting. At the end of the day, the station shuts down after the last train pulls into the platform, and you are still waiting. You fall asleep on the bench, waiting until the morning, till you wake to the sounds of conductors and busy people rushing to their destinations.

You stretch your arms and legs, counting your change and trying to decide whether or not to buy some breakfast and a cup of coffee, unsure if it will be enough to last you till you get to your destination.

Imagine being there for days, repeating this cycle, just waiting patiently, silently for a train, meanwhile you have no idea where you are going. If you have no idea of where you are going, how do you know what train you need to get on, or if you even need a train?

Without a clear vision, without knowing where you are going, you will waste your time waiting on an opportunity that is constantly passing you by.

Know what you are going after and be clear on your direction.

Ruth had a vision. Naomi gave Ruth the plan, she told her, "It's time to settle down, it's time to get you a permanent home, but it cannot be just any home. The vision is for you to marry Boaz."

While we wait on God, the first thing we must really pay attention to do is be clear on our purpose.

Write your vision down, refine it, make it clear, then you can begin to get ready for what God has in store for you.

2. The Principle of Washing Yourself

It is possible to be healed and delivered from something and still be affected by the effects of what you went through. We will never be ready for what God has for us now if the past is still actively driving our lives. Naomi told Ruth to take a bath, to wash off the dirt and dust and baggage that came with her daily activities.

As we go through life, things may have a way of sticking to us until we begin to look like what we have been through. However, we cannot go forward until we allow the Word of God to cleanse clinging issues from our lives. There would be no difference in our encounters with opportunity until we stop looking like where we have been and start looking like where we are going.

3. The Principle of an Adjusted Attitude

Naomi instructed Ruth to put on perfume, to try a new fragrance, to affect people's encounter of her by influencing their experience pleasantly. For what she was going to experience, a new countenance was crucial.

Learn to adjust your attitude.

Our attitudes are things that can be put on. Regardless of whether we feel like it in the moment, we must learn to put on the right attitude. Without the right attitude, we will not attract the blessings of God. Nobody wants to be around someone with a bad attitude. Smile, be pleasant, polite, optimistic, determined.

Do not allow the situation to determine your attitude. Purposely decide to put it on.

4. The Principle of Presentation

In preparation for our destination, we need to present ourselves as though we are already there. It may not have happened yet, but we need to be prepared for what God has for us. No one goes on a date and waits till they get to the fancy restaurant before they begin to change their clothes; they get ready at home, getting dressed for where they are going, so that when they get there, they fit in.

A prepared person in the right place and at the right time is a person ready for God's blessing. As we wait for what God has for us, this is an opportunity to look ahead and get ready for the things that we have not yet seen or heard, for the things that God has for us.

5. The Principle of Placement

It is dangerous to stay too long in a place you are over-dressed for.

When we start moving into our destiny, we will some-times feel out of place and uncomfortable because we are coming from a place we were overdressed for, to a place we have never been before. In these times, we need to get ourselves situated in the right place.

There are certain places where things happen and in order to step into our divine destiny, we need to be in the right place. No matter how packed and prepared you are, you cannot catch a train from your bedroom.

Naomi told Ruth where and when to go to Boaz. Life is not going to come and find us; we need to situate ourselves in the place God has preordained for us to meet with our destiny. We must step out of our comfort zones and go to where we need to be.

6. The Principle of Divine Timing

When we get in the place that God wants us to be, we mustn't try to make things happen ourselves, or to force things to happen. We need to be prepared, but we must learn to wait, because God would be the one to open the doors for us. We mustn't try to assist God; He does not need our help!

There is a time for everything, and God makes all things beautiful at the right time. If we try to force something to happen before it is time, we will end up creating a disaster.

Naomi advised Ruth of not just the place, but also the time. Timing is very important. We may be ready for our journey, be at the right station and at the right platform, but if we are there at the wrong time, the whole journey may change.

7. The Principle of Observation

There are a lot of things we see but do not take notice of and later, we come to realise that the one little detail we glossed over was actually very important. It is a principle that affects the course of our lives, the principle of observation.

People have lost their lives because they or someone else, failed to observe a minor error which eventually escalated. Other people have become a huge success because they noticed something that others did not. A lot of the book of Proverbs was written based on someone's observations. This teaches us that a lot of wisdom comes through observation.

Ruth noticed when and where Boaz lay. A lot of times, we fail to notice the opportunities and open doors God puts in front of us because we do not think it is important.

From now on, start to notice the things going on around you.

8. The Principle of Instruction

Ruth followed instructions. There is almost nothing more important or influential during our lives than our decision to follow certain instructions. That is the power in having and trusting a mentor.

A lot of people despise instruction because they feel they are being controlled and, in a streak of rebellion, want to break free and be independent. There is nothing wrong with being different, but the road to success is rough and bumpy. As such, instructions will help reduce the number of troubles we may have to face.

Listening to and obeying someone who has gone ahead of and can see further than us will always propel us forward.

Learning from the experiences of others is even more crucial than learning from your own, so endeavour to treasure wise counsel when it is given and begin to obey it once you have it.

9. The Principle of Believing in Divine Destiny

Ruth went out to look for a job and her hap was to end up finding a job in her husband's kinsman's company. These happenstances are not accidents. Do not take coincidences for granted. It is not by accident that we the meet people we do at a certain place or encounter them in a certain way.

There is no such thing as a coincidence.

Do not take coincidences for granted. Believe in the grace of God and the hand of God directing your paths as you go along.

It was not by chance that Ruth ended up working on Boaz's land. When God brings you into contact or relation with someone in any way, do not take it for granted.

Sometimes, you may never know, the person you are destined to be with is just three people away, and how you relate with those people in between you and them will determine and affect a lot.

Do not take people for granted.

10. The Principle of Being Prepared to do Menial Jobs

Ruth was not ashamed to do menial jobs. In those days, the Lord had given a law that anyone with land was not supposed to harvest everything, they were to leave some around for the poor and widowed to glean (Deuteronomy 24:21, Leviticus 19:10).

Ruth was not ashamed to do this job. She understood that this was the way God had provided for her and her kind (widows) to survive and she went out to make use of it.

As we wait on God and search for Him, we should be prepared to do what we deem to be menial jobs in His house, just as Ruth was prepared to glean behind the reapers and provide for Naomi. Often, the seemingly little things we must do are the small cracks we slip through into our greatness.

WAITING ON GOD

More importantly, as we wait, we must not stop seeking God. Seek Him consistently through our prayer and worship, getting to know Him more through His Word.

In consistently seeking the face of God and not just His hand (power, provision, and any other benefits) in the times of waiting, saturating ourselves in His Word and doing what He says, we will begin to see the Lord manifest Himself to us in unimaginable ways.

It is in those moments, we will come to realise that He has been with us all along and even when it felt like we were alone and searching, He never left us. He was right there with us.

This is not the end of the journey, for to think this journey has an end is to think we can know God in totality. We will come to understand that the more of Him we know, the more we realise that we really do not know Him entirely for there is so much more to experience.

You will begin to walk with God on a deeper level, hungering and thirsting for more intimacy and seeking Him with greater zeal and passion until you are consumed by who He is.

★★★

Enter a covenant today to seek the Lord God of Israel, to follow Him and to love and serve Him by doing the same to those He has brought our way.

The journey may be long and hard, and there will be times when our faith falters, but we must keep our eyes fixed on the author and finisher of our faith.

After we have been tested and our hearts have been tried, if we can hold on to these principles and keep seeking God with a pure heart, obeying His Word in faith, He will surely manifest Himself to us as a friend like no other.

SHOW ME YOUR GLORY

THE HAND OF DAVID

"And it came to pass, when the evil spirit from God was upon Saul, that David took an harp, and played with his hand: so Saul was refreshed, and was well, and the evil spirit departed from him."

-1 Samuel 16:23

The above verse tells us David took an (a) harp, not his harp. It is said that the harp, the lute and the cithern are similar and that David's harp in fact, seemed to be more of a lyre than an actual harp.

This is significant because it means that, as much as it was the harp he played, it was not the harp that mattered. It was not a particular harp that mattered.

We ought to get it out of our minds that it is playing a particular musical instrument that matters and stop thinking that it is a particular brand, model or make of our instrument that really makes the difference.

Here, we see clearly that David's harp was probably not even a harp, and there was actually no particular one he favoured.

I'm not implying that these things are not important or that they don't have an impact, what I am saying is that there was more to

David's playing than the instrument he used. His playing was not determined by his instrument. The effect of his playing was determined by more than what he played.

The Bible tells us that David played with his hand. He did not just play; he played it with his hand. The Bible will not state something as obvious as that if there was no significance in it being stated, if God wasn't emphasising something. I believe God doesn't waste words, which could only mean He was making a point: David's playing with his hand is significant.

The word translated as "Hand" is from the Hebrew word "*yād*", which is also interpreted as;

1. Power
2. Figure of control
3. Care
4. Strength
5. Direction

The word "yād" is also translated in some verses as: "Coast, consecrate, dominion, ministry, wait on, work, and service."

From this, we understand that David played the harp with care and control: he played it with direction, with strength and with power.

THE SIGNIFICANCE OF THE HAND OF DAVID

1. The hand of David signifies consecration

> "And it came to pass, when the evil spirit from God was upon Saul, that David took a harp, and played with his hand: so Saul was refreshed, and was well, and the evil spirit departed from him."
>
> -1 Samuel 16:23

To consecrate is to ordain for the service of God. When David played the harp with his hand, it meant that he wasn't just playing for the fun of it. He wasn't making music with the harp simply because he knew how to or because he enjoyed it, he was consecrating to the priestly office whoever he was playing to or for.

God instructed Moses to consecrate Aaron to be a priest in order that Aaron may stand in His presence and offer a service unto Him. This act of consecration was what David performed when he played with his hand.

He played to consecrate Saul for the service of God and that is why when he played, the Bible records that the evil spirit departed from Saul.

2. The hand of David signifies ministry

> "And David came to Saul, and stood before him: and he loved him greatly; and he became his armour bearer. And Saul sent to Jesse, saying, Let David, I pray thee, stand before me; for he hath found favour in my sight."
>
> -1 Samuel 16:21-22

The dictionary defines a *ministry* as "a spiritual work or service of any Christian or group of Christians." It is not a game or a hobby, it is work.

When David played with his hand, he wasn't playing it for recreational purposes, he was playing it as work, as his job, as his ministry. He played with his hand when he stood to do the job God had employed him to do.

David understood that a job required him to carry out more than one activity to get it done. Playing the harp was one of the activities that his job comprised of. He was employed to stand before the king, and one of his job specifications was to bear his armour, another was to play the harp to Saul.

Work is activity involving mental and physical effort done to achieve a purpose or result. He played with purpose, he played with direction, and he had an aim when he played.

David did not stop playing for Saul when times were hard, he did not play for Saul only when it was convenient for him or only when he felt like it. He did not quit even after Saul had thrown a spear at him because he understood that it was work he had been given to do and he carried out his task with that in mind.

3. The hand of David signifies power

> "And the Lord said to Satan, "Behold, all that he has is in your hand. Only against him do not stretch out your hand." So Satan

went out from the presence of the Lord."

- Job 1:12 (English Standard Version)

Power can be defined as the capacity or ability to direct or influence the behaviour of others or the course of events. It is a right that is given or delegated to a person of authority.

David played with an authority that was given or delegated to him by someone else to influence Saul's behaviour.

Playing with his hand, he was playing under a delegated authority to influence; change the course of events and the behaviour of Saul, and not just to entertain him.

Power has two facets to it: ability and authority. The fact that one can do a thing doesn't mean that they have the authority to do it.

The reverse is also true; because one may have the authority to do something, it doesn't necessarily mean they can. Power is a combination of both ability and authority.

David had the ability to play before kings and, when Saul appointed him as a servant in his court, he then received the authority to do so.

We mustn't stop at developing our ability to do certain things, we ought to go further to receive the corresponding authority necessary to successfully implement our gifts and abilities.

There's no better person to authorize us than God himself. When God gives us the ability to do something, He will cause us to have favour in the eyes of those who can authorize us.

After Saul's disobedience, God sent Samuel to anoint David to be the king of Israel. David was marked out and authorized by God and that caused him to find favour in the presence of Saul.

When Satan went to God and God pointed out Job to him, he had the ability to destroy all Job had and to torment him, but he had no power to go ahead and do it until he had been authorized by God to do so.

To truly have power, we need to develop the ability and receive the authority to do whatever it is we want to do.

EIGHT CHARACTERISTICS OF DAVID

> *"but I have chosen Jerusalem, that my name might be there; and have chosen David to be over my people Israel."*
>
> *- 2 Chronicles 6:6*

We know that David was a harpist, so let's take a look at what type of harpist he was.

The following are some characteristics of David as listed in scripture.

1. David was a cunning player

> *"Let our lord now command thy servants, which are before thee, to seek out a man, who is a cunning player on an harp..."*
>
> *-1 Samuel 16:16*

A cunning player is someone who plays with skill, someone who really knows and understands the intricate parts of music and the instrument they are playing.

Yāda, translated to the word cunning, ranges in meaning from the mere acquisition and understanding of information to intimacy in relationship, including some sexual relations. It is also translated as skilful in Daniel 1:4.

We should study and acquire knowledge on doing whatever it is that we do. Take lessons if necessary to learn all we can in our chosen fields.

2. David could play well

> *"And Saul said unto his servants, Provide me now a man that can play well, and bring him to me."*
>
> *-1 Samuel 16:17*

Playing well implies that the way one plays is good and pleasing, that one plays the right thing and that the song, or music, is made successful by the way one plays.

One should be able to control and affect emotions using music. Our playing ought to make a difference by bringing something of oneself to the music.

To measure how successful a thing is, it must have achieved a certain aim.

To be right, it must have hit a certain standard. We are all aware that what is right to you might not necessarily be right to me.

To play well means to meet the outcome set by whoever has commissioned you to do so, and if that person is God, then He is the one who sets the standards which you are to meet.

3. David was a son

> *"Then answered one of the servants, and said, Behold, I have seen a son of Jesse the Bethlehemite..."*
>
> -1 Samuel 16:18

A boy is different from a man, and a man is different from a father, who is also different from a son. A son can be defined as the product of a particular person, influence, or environment.

Being a son (referring to both genders in this context) means one comes from somewhere.

One has a reference point and did not just fall out of the sky. Being a son signifies being under authority. It means that one is controllable (responsible to another). It means that one can be vouched for.

In biblical days, sons were disowned if they dis-honoured their parents and taken out and stoned if they were stubborn. The fact that someone was referred to as the son of another showed that they were an honourable and responsible person.

There are several factors that signify sonship.

God gives fathers to everyone because He will never leave His children fatherless. However, even though God has given this gift to everyone, it's up to each of us to receive this great and wonderful gift.

People are not automatically receptive of others and should learn how to receive the gift of God to us in the form of a Father.

WHAT IT MEANS TO RECEIVE

Take Delivery Of

"He came unto his own, and his own received him not. But as many as received him, to them gave he power to become the sons of God, even to them that believe on his name:"

-John 1:11-12

When a delivery comes for you, you would need to answer the door and get the parcel; you need to receive the parcel. The parcel has been brought to your door, but you need to collect it because it's pretty much illegal for the postman to force the parcel on you or break into your house to deliver it.

Some people don't receive parcels, either because they are not expecting them, or they do not want them.

THE UNEXPECTED DELIVERY

One fine autumn evening, after the heavy showers had died down, I decided to take a walk. I geared up and readied myself, called out my greetings to the family to let them know I was heading out, then made my way to the front door.

I opened it to find, to my surprise, three large parcels and a smaller one sitting at the doorstep, all soaked through. I hurriedly brought them in and opened them up to make sure none of the items had sustained any water damage.

Luckily, they hadn't.

I wasn't expecting those parcels so, if I hadn't decided to take a walk, they would have sat outside in rain until the next day.

The gifts of God are just like parcels that have been delivered to your doorstep. You now need to receive them.

When God brings a father into our lives, it's then up to us to accept that this is the parcel for us. Learn to identify and accept the people God brings into your life as fathers.

Consent to hear

"My son, hear the instruction of thy father, and forsake not the law of thy mother:"

-Proverbs 1:8

A father is someone we choose to listen to. It's a choice we need to make to listen to what our fathers say. If we choose to listen to our father's instruction, we have in effect, received them. Decide today who you are going to listen to and actively move to listen to that person.

Respond to something in a specified way

"Children, obey your parents in the Lord: for this is right. Honour thy father and mother; which is the first commandment with promise; That it may be well with thee, and thou mayest live long on the earth."

-Ephesians 6:1-3

There is a way a child ought to respond to a father and that is in obedience and honour. In obeying and honouring the fathers God has given us, we are receiving them.

Widely accept as authoritative and true

"And what he hath seen and heard, that he testifieth; and no man receiveth his testimony. He that hath received his testimony hath set to his seal that God is true."

-John 3:32-33

My mother is always right. Her mind is like an encyclopaedia! I actually ask her things before I ask the internet (shocking, I know). A father figure in a certain area of your life will often be an authority in that area, field, or speciality. There are many ways to do things, we all know that. So, when God sends you a father, that individual will guide you in the way they know and have mastered. This doesn't negate other routes or paths; it just makes yours easier.

If we don't believe in the fathers God has given us and we don't accept their authority over our lives as final, we have rejected them.

To receive a father is to accept that their word is final and to believe in them and in their authority, even when it goes against our will or our reasoning (so long as it doesn't go against the principles and the Word of God).

This doesn't mean fathers are always perfect or always right (like my mother), it just means that God will bless and cover us when we bring ourselves under the authority he has provided for us.

4. David was a mighty valiant man

> *"... and a mighty valiant man..."*
>
> -1 Samuel 16:18

A valiant person is one who shows courage or determination.

David was not afraid to venture into the unknown. He was not afraid to try new things and in whatever he did, he always did it with the mind to come out on top. He did not waver in his purpose; he did not get distracted. David, instead, focused and worked hard and fearlessly at what he did.

We mustn't get scared to try new things. We ought to be focused and determined with great courage.

5. David was a man of war

> *"... and a man of war..."*
>
> -1 Samuel 16:18

Being a man of war is different from being a soldier.

David was not a soldier. I personally don't think he was even old enough to be in the army at that time. But David was a man of battle. He fought.

He didn't give in to circumstances; he didn't fall and accept his fate. He was a fighter.

He battled to achieve what he believed. He didn't sit and let lions and bears walk all over him, he fought to protect what was rightfully his.

To be people with a fighting spirit, we ought not to let things defeat us and let the devil walk all over us. To be a man of battle means to stand up for what you believe in and even if you're beaten, you go down fighting.

David wasn't a pushover. He wasn't rude or disrespectful about it either; he just wasn't going to get kicked about or let people and circumstances get him down.

We should learn to be fighters; we should learn to be strong and not let people or what they say and do, get us down.

Please, don't misunderstand me. I am not propagating violence. Do not take this too literally and go about hitting people on the playground.

We need to be mentally and emotionally tough and battle for our own place in the Kingdom (Matthew 11:12). There is a certain violence (spiritual, mental and emotional strength) we need to have in order to make it as Christians.

David was a fighter and that helped him in life.

He was able to overcome his enemies and still stay the course even when his situation seemed hopeless because the Lord was his strength. In the same way, the Holy Spirit will give us strength to overcome.

6. David was prudent in matters

> *"... and prudent in matters..."*
>
> *-1 Samuel 16:18*

To be prudent is to have a certain level or depth of understanding; to understand something to the point of making things happen; to have understanding to be able to realize things or make things become real. It is the practical application of what you know in the right way and at the right time.

There are things that must be done that we shouldn't have to be told. We should be able to take up things and learn and understand them quickly.

7. A comely person

> *"... and a comely person..."*
>
> *-1 Samuel 16:18*

A comely person is a beautiful person or a fine-looking person. You may not have been born beautiful in your eyes, you may not be Mr. or Miss Universe, or have the best figure, but how you present yourself makes a huge difference to everything.

Putting some care in our physical appearance affects the way people receive and treat us. We ought to learn to present ourselves well.

One doesn't necessarily need to follow fashion trends; one only need to take care of oneself and appearance. If we need to hit the gym, start working out, go on a diet (my personal favourite), do it.

Invest in your appearance. This means different things to different people. To some, it means invest in good quality clothes, to others, it may mean better personal hygiene or dental care.

Investing in your appearance doesn't necessarily mean one must become a doll, just present yourself the way you want to feel. If you want to feel good and confident, find what that means to you and present yourself in that way.

Queen Esther took time to look good. David was described in the Bible as someone who was fine-looking, someone who was good to look at.

Being Christians doesn't mean we can't have a good sense of style or taste; it doesn't mean we should not look good.

8. The Lord is with him

> *"... and the Lord is with him."*
>
> *-1 Samuel 16:18*

The presence of The Lord is a very important factor. What made David special was that God was with him. We can work on all the other factors and acquire them ourselves, but one doesn't just acquire the presence of the Almighty God.

For God to decide to come and be with us means a lot. It's not something that we do; it's something that He does. In a certain sense, no one can make you come to be with them; you must want to, and then go to be with them. It's a matter of your will. How much more, the Ever-living God?

We can't force or fake the presence of God. If God is with us, He is with us, and if He is not, He is not. Because God is okay with or has endorsed what we're doing, that doesn't automatically mean He is with us.

THE MEANING OF THE PRESENCE

"And he said, My presence shall go with thee, and I will give thee rest."

- Exodus 33:14

When the presence of The Lord is with a person, it means that God has come to them. He has come into their situation or circumstance. He has come to *be* where they are. (See John 14:23-26.)

There are different dimensions of the Presence, and this is so for different reasons. God has a reason for everything He does and there are two main biblical reasons why God comes to be with people.

One is for fellowship, for company. God comes to people because He enjoys fellowship. He loves His people and loves to be with them, but He cannot dwell in sin. That's why Jesus said that God will come to those who keep His words.

The second reason, which I believe has its root in the first, is because He has a job or work to do with you, or for you to do for Him. I say that this reason stems from the first reason because God usually gives tasks to people He trusts and knows will do them.

Sometimes, it works the other way around where God gives someone the task to do and through working with the person, develops a certain kind of relationship with them. In such a case, it's not that God gets to know the person better, but that person gets to know Him better and in doing so, they strengthen their faith and go where He leads or directs.

These here are different levels or dimensions of the presence of the Lord which I have found in the Bible. They may be referred to differently by other people but, simply because it gives a clearer understanding and is a lot easier to remember, I personally like to refer to them as *the Eden dimension* and *the Wilderness dimension*.

1. The Eden dimension

"and they heard the voice of the Lord walking in the garden in the cool of the day..."

-Genesis 3:8

This is the dimension where The Lord comes to be with us at certain times for fellowship. At these times, The Lord speaks to us and fellowships with us, teaching us things and showing us things.

It is the same experience the disciples had with Jesus on the road to Emmaus in Luke 24. It is when the presence of God is experienced mainly for fellowship and teaching.

This is commonly where people can and will develop a deeper relationship with God.

When God called Moses and sent him to deliver His people from Egypt, Moses didn't really know God all that well. It wasn't up until Exodus 34, that Moses experienced this dimension of the presence where God fellowshipped with him on the mountain, teaching and showing him things.

It was during these 40-day encounters that he allegedly wrote the book of Genesis. This is when God revealed to him what happened in Eden and how the fellowship they were having was the same fellowship that He intended to have with man when He created him.

When this dimension of the presence is with us, we hear the Lord speaking to us, teaching us things, showing us things and explaining things to us. God fellowships with us like His friends.

I believe this is the primary dimension of the presence of God that is intended for every Christian is to walk in. This is the most basic relationship we are to have with the Lord as this was the level God created man to start from, this is the ground zero of our relationship with God.

2. The Wilderness dimension

> *"For wherein shall it be known here that I and thy people have found grace in thy sight? Is it not in that thou goest with us? so shall we be separated, I and thy people, from all the people that are upon*

the face of the earth."

-Exodus 33:16

In the wilderness, the Lord comes to abide with us. He comes to stay, remain, dwell, rest, live with us. It means that He is always around and has a place prepared specially for Him with us.

It was in such a place that God instructed Moses to build a tabernacle for Him to dwell in so that He could be with His people. (See Exodus 34.)

In this dimension of the presence, God remains/rests upon a person. He doesn't come to visit occasionally; He comes to live with them. They become His home, His resting place.

His presence becomes their signature to the point that when people see that person, they don't see them anymore, they see God's presence. In this dimension, He becomes the landlord of their life, and they become the tenant.

In this dimension, they are set apart solely and completely for Him and for His purpose.

In the Eden dimension, God visits, spends time and fellowships with us and then steps back and allows us to do our thing, but in this wilderness dimension, God lives with us. He doesn't step back to anywhere, He remains, living our life through us. He almost literally possesses us.

This is the dimension of His presence we all need to have.

Most often, we will see that the people who walk in this dimension are people who have yielded themselves totally to the Holy Spirit. God usually comes in this dimension to those He favours, and He often favours people by giving them a special job to do for Him.

The more He has favoured a person, the more special the job He gives them.

When the Lord came to be with Mary, to come to the earth through her and to live in her house, the angel told her that it's because she was highly favoured among women (Luke 1:28).

When the Lord came to be with Noah and give him the task of building the arc, the Bible says that Noah found grace (favour) in the sight of the Lord (Genesis 6:8).

When God called Moses and sent him to Egypt to deliver the Israelites, the Bible records that it was because he had found grace (favour) in the sight of the Lord. (See Exodus 33:12-18.)

The people who have found favour or grace in the eyes of the Lord are the people He gives very sensitive and seemingly impossible tasks to do. One trademark of these tasks is that they demand one's life. It takes their whole life to achieve it.

For this fact, God must live and work through them to achieve the impossible. God must permanently be with them because every second of their lives, every decision they take, every move they make is very important.

Imagine Mary who was meant to bring up the Child Jesus and only had occasional visits from The Lord, how on earth would she be able to bring up the Messiah, the saviour of the world, without Gods permanent help and input?

So, we will see that we walk in this dimension because the Father has something for us to do, because He has given us a special task that requires Him to be on the scene 24/7. Even the evil spirits knew that when Jesus appeared on the scene, it was because there was something to be done there.

Therefore, they always asked Him, "What do you want? Why are you here?" They understood that His presence meant business. (See Matthew 8:29, Mark 1:24, Mark 5:7, Luke 1:28.)

SIGNS OF THE PRESENCE OF GOD

"God answered, "I will be with you. And this is your sign that I am the one who has sent you..."

- Exodus 3:12 (New Living Translation)

It is possible to know when the presence of The Lord is upon you or anyone else. There are tell-tale signs, certain things which happen to let you know that The Lord is present. I have stated a few signs, a few ways to help one identify when The Lord is present.

1. The voice of God *(John 14:25)*

When God's presence is with you, you will hear His voice. The Spirit of God will speak to you when He is with you.

The clearest indicator that God is with you is that He speaks to you.

2. The provision/influence of the Spirit *(Galatians 5:22-25)*

When God is with you, He influences you. He does things and makes a difference in your life.

For a few years, I lived with a dear friend of mine and whenever she was not around, her cooking, cleaning, and tidying was missed.

The people you spend time with and keep round you will affect the way you behave. When the presence of God is in your life then He will affect the way you behave. He will influence you.

When someone is around, there are certain things that they do for you that you will notice the absence of when their presence is gone. (See Isaiah 45:2-3.)

When I was much younger, I had an aunt who often brought me chocolate when we met. Aunty Bisi provided me with more than chocolate, I saw her as a rock to hold on to in hard times, and I believe she provided me with a spiritual covering and an emotional stability.

When she died, I lost more than the chocolate she gave me. I lost that covering, I lost that stability, and it really affected the way the next few years of my life turned out. When God's presence leaves you, you lose His influence and His provision in your life.

3). A feeling, knowing or sensing of His presence *(Job 23:8-10)*
When someone is around, you feel their presence. They don't have to do anything, but you just know they are there. Whenever my friend with whom I lived would travel, I felt her absence. Even though things went on as normal, I felt alone at home because she wasn't around.

We hardly did anything together when she was around, but I still felt like I was not alone simply because she was there. Sometimes, just being there makes a whole lot of difference. When God is around, you will sense His presence with you, you will know you are not alone, and it will make a great difference.

When God anoints you, He makes you a place He can come and be. He makes you holy so you can carry His presence. The Ark of God was anointed so that God's presence could remain there. When God anoints you, He is making you a modern-day Ark to carry His presence (see Exodus 40).

When God commanded that the children of Israel should make Him a sanctuary, it was because He had promised them His presence but because He is HOLY, He needed a holy place to dwell in when He came to dwell among them.

> *"And they made the plate of the holy crown of pure gold, and wrote upon it a writing, like to the engravings of a signet, HOLINESS TO THE Lord."*
>
> *-Exodus 39:30*

The anointing sanctifies, it makes you Holy so that God's presence can descend upon you. The Spirit of the Lord could rest upon Jesus because he had been anointed. He had been made holy and sanctified by the anointing of the Holy Spirit.

When the Lord anoints you, He gives you His Holy Spirit who teaches you and leads you into all truth. The Holy Spirit reminds you of all that Jesus has said, teaches you His words, and leads you to walk in it. (See John 14:23-26.)

This way, you keep the words of Jesus and so Jesus comes with the

Father to make their abode with you.

Sadly, most Christians nowadays are content with just having the Holy Spirit remind them of the words of Jesus or teach them His words. Not many follow His leading to get to the point of keeping the words of Christ and therefore, only a few ever get to the place where Jesus and the Father actually come and dwell with them.

THE ANOINTING

"The Spirit of the Lord is upon me, because he hath anointed me…"

-Luke 4:18

In this scripture, Jesus was reading from Isaiah 61:1-2.

The word "Anointed" is in Hebrew, a verb derived from the noun "Anointing."

The anointing was first mentioned in the Bible in Exodus 25 when God called Moses to come up into the cloud so He would show him what to teach the people.

God told Moses about the Anointing oil that he would use to consecrate priests and sanctify them to minister unto Him in the priest's office.

"And thou shalt put them upon Aaron thy brother, and his sons with him; and shalt anoint them, and consecrate them, and sanctify them, that they may minister unto me in the priest's office."

-Exodus 28:41

This noun, anointing, refers to the oil. It is translated from the Hebrew to mean the "anointing oil, usually referring to pouring or smearing sacred oil on a person in a ceremony of dedication, possibly symbolising divine empowering to accomplish a task or office."

When God established the anointing, nobody else was allowed to mix it, or mix anything even like it, neither was anyone allowed to use it to anoint anybody except by God's instruction. Exodus 25-30 gives a lot of details on the anointing, it's purpose and God's instructions on how it should be carried out.

The anointing oil was and is special because it served a single purpose: the anointing oil was and is a holy oil used for sanctification.

To be holy is to be set apart as dedicated to God. The "holy of holies" is a most holy place, set apart exclusively for the presence of God, with very limited high priestly access.

To sanctify means to be dedicated, consecrated, and set apart as dedicated to God.

The anointing oil is the medium God used to sanctify and set people and things apart exclusively for His presence.

WHAT IT MEANS TO BE ANOINTED

It means:

1. He is choosing you
2. He sets you apart from everyone else
3. He has made you His own, marked out especially for Him
4. He is coming to be with you

5. He wants to give you a specific task to perform

When God anoints someone, there are two distinct facets of the anointing: the presence of God and the work of God.

THE PRESENCE

1. When God anointed DAVID, the Bible states that God was with him (*1 Samuel 16:13-18*)
2. When God anointed ELISHA, the Bible says that God was with him (*2 Kings 3:14*)
3. When God anointed SAMUEL, the Bible says that God was with him (*1 Samuel 3:19*)
4. When God anointed JOSHUA, the Bible says that God was with him (*Deuteronomy 31:7-9*)
5. When God anointed JESUS, the Bible says that God was with Him (*John 3:1-2, Acts 10:38*)
6. When God anointed MOSES, His presence was with him (*Exodus 33:14*)

THE WORK

1. When God called Moses, He told Moses to anoint Aaron and his sons to minister to Him in the priest's office (*Exodus 30:30*)
2. When God anointed Jesus, He gave him to preach the gospel to

the poor, heal the broken-hearted, preach deliverance to the captives and recovery of sight to the blind, set at liberty them that were bruised, preach the acceptable year of the Lord (*Luke 4:18-19*)

3. When God sent Samuel, He told Samuel to anoint Saul to deliver His people from the hands of the philistines (*1 Samuel 9:16-17*)
4. When God called Elijah, He sent Elijah to anoint Elisha as a prophet to continue the work he was doing when he was gone (*1 Kings 19:16*)
5. When God anointed Joshua, God gave him the task of leading the children of Israel to possess the promised land (*Deuteronomy 31:7-8*)
6. When God anointed the disciples, He gave them a specific task to be witnesses (*Acts 1:8*)

God is anointing you for a specific purpose. God is making you holy so He can come and be with you.

FORTY DAYS IN HIS PRESENCE

"And it came to pass, when Moses came down from mount Sinai with the two tablets of testimony in Moses' hand, when he came down from the mount, that Moses wist not that the skin of his face shone while he talked with him."

- Exodus 34:29

Moses had two 40-day encounters with God. The first time was when God called him and assigned him to teach the people of Israel. That was when God gave him the 10 commandments which he broke when the children of Israel had made a golden calf to worship.

When he went up the mountain at this time, Joshua went with him (Exodus 24:12-18). The second time Moses went up the Mountain, he went alone. He went before God and was there 40 days. (Exodus 34:1-28).

These 40 days, God was answering Moses's prayer. Moses had prayed in the tabernacle for something specific and God used those 40 days to answer it.

THE PRAYERS OF MOSES.

In Exodus 33:13-18, Moses prayed to God for three specific things. I call these *the prayers of Moses*. These revolutionary, lifechanging prayers are listed as:

1. Show me your way
    a. That I may know you
    b. That I may find favour in your sight
2. Consider that this nation is your people
3. Show me your glory (your self)

Moses was asking for the presence of God. He wanted God to be with him. He wanted to know the ways of God so that God's presence would remain with him. He wanted to know God so that God would remain with him.

He wanted to find grace in the sight of God so that the presence of God would not depart from him. He wanted God to acknowledge and receive the people so that God's presence would remain with them. He wanted to see the Glory of God.

> *"And he said, I beseech thee, shew me thy glory."*
>
> *-Exodus 33:18*

The *glory* referred to in that verse is the Hebrew word "Kābôd." It is a title for God, focusing on His splendour and high status; "my glory" means "myself."

THE PURPOSE OF THE PRESENCE

"And he said, Certainly I will be with thee..."

– Exodus 3:12

God anoints people so that His Spirit can come upon them. So why do we need the presence of The Lord? Why do we need His presence upon us constantly? Why can't we just enjoy the presence of God occasionally when He comes to fellowship?

The reason is because God has called us for a specific task which we have no hope of accomplishing without Him. A more popular way to phrase this is, without him, we can do nothing (John 15:5).

When Moses was in Egypt and the wilderness doing all sorts of things, he didn't need the presence of God, he didn't even know God. But when God called him and gave him a job to do, he said that he's not going to do anything without the presence of God.

When God gave Moses something to do, when God revealed to Moses his calling, Moses would not do the work without God's presence. God asked Moses to make the tabernacle so that His presence will remain with them just as He promised. (See Exodus 3:1-

12, 33:12-16.)

Here are some reasons why the presence of God is so important for the work He gives you to do:

1. The presence of the Lord is a sign that we have found grace in God's sight

The gifts and the calling of God are without repentance. If God calls us to do something or gives us a gift, He doesn't take it back. We could be operating in the gifts and still walking in the calling of God but that doesn't mean that God is happy with us. The presence of God is a clear sign that God is happy with us.

When the children of Israel angered God, Moses would not continue to operate in the calling of God because God was not happy with them.

God was going to send an angel to go with them, but Moses blatantly refused to follow the angel, he completely refused to move if God was not going to go with them. He was not going to continue the journey if God was not pleased with them. If God was not coming, he was not going. (See Exodus 33:15-16.)

King Saul was a person who God was angry with, and so removed His presence from, when he had sinned through disobedience. God was angry with Saul but still left him as the king of Israel.

Saul probably didn't understand the importance of the presence of God or, like many people do, thought that a sign of God being pleased with him was the fact that he wasn't removed from his position; God hadn't taken back what He had given.

We must understand that God doesn't behave like men. If a man is angry with you, most times they show it by taking back all that they've given you.

When couples divorce, they contend over property and possessions and try to take back as much as is equivalent to their investment in the relationship. God doesn't behave like that. He's infinite with an infinite number of resources and doesn't have to take back anything to still be able to go on.

His investment in you does not in any way deplete Him or His resources and so He doesn't take back the gifts and callings. He doesn't uproot seeds He has already planted; He just turns away.

Saul was begging not to be removed from the office God had given him because he thought that the people would know God was not pleased with him if he lost his office. (See 1 Samuel 15:24-35.)

King David, on the other hand, understood the importance of the presence of God. He understood that the cardinal sign that God is happy with you is the fact that He stays with you.

When David sinned against God and a prophet was sent to him to let him know that God was not pleased, he did not ask for the kingdom to remain with him, he asked for the presence to remain with him. (See 2 Samuel 12.)

He understood that sin defiles and the Spirit of God is HOLY and therefore cannot dwell where sin is, that is why he repented of what he did.

> *"Hide thy face from my sins, and blot out all mine iniquities. Create in me a clean heart, O God; and renew a right spirit within me. Cast me not away from thy presence; and take not thy holy spirit from me. Restore unto me the joy of thy salvation; and uphold me with thy free spirit."*
>
> *-Psalms 51:9-12*

King David was someone who was hyper-vigilant about sin and iniquity because he was very conscious of the presence of God. He did all he could to keep the laws of God and to obey Him because he valued the presence of God even more than the work that God had given him to do. (See Psalms 18:19-23.)

A lot of times, we fall into the trap of the enemy and begin to esteem the work of God above His presence and that's a big and very dangerous mistake. This mistake is one that even Jesus has said will cost some people their salvation (Matthew 7:21-23). It comes as no shock that Moses prayed "... Shew me now thy way, that I may know thee, that I may find grace in thy sight..." (Exodus 33:13).

2. The presence of the Lord separates us and makes us different from everyone else

It's the presence of God that makes the difference. If one is to do a particular work for God, what's the difference between them and someone else who is doing the same thing? (Exodus 33:15-16).

I play the piano and I know quite a lot of people who play much better than me, so what makes the difference between my music and theirs? It's because God is with me.

His presence is with me, and I am conscious of the fact that if He were ever to leave me, I'd be less than ordinary. I have seen a practical difference between when I do things for God on my own and when I do it with His presence with me.

David was a skilled harpist. He was very talented, and his music was pleasant to listen to. But I don't believe that David was one-of-a-kind when it came to skills. I'm sure there were people who could match him in skill, exposure and even maturity. What made the difference in David's playing—and why it was that when he played demons fled—was because God was with him.

The thing about his playing that made him play for kings to receive their healing was the presence! (See 1 Samuel 16:14-23).

3. The presence of the Lord causes us to speak the Word of God with boldness

> *"And when they had prayed, the place was shaken where they were assembled together; and they were all filled with the Holy Ghost, and they spake the word of God with boldness."*
>
> *-Acts 4:31*

Many times, people are scared to do things on their own. They feel more confident when someone is with them, most especially when it's the person that sent them.

My younger brother made a profound statement once. He said to me, "people who 'say it as it is' only do so when they are not alone." Though this is not a proven fact, and it may not always be the case, but it really struck me.

A lot of people who pride themselves in saying things as they are or giving people "a piece of their minds" will hardly ever do so when they are alone or when they have no one supporting their cause.

They often name-drop to support their allegations. It gives them confidence to know that they are not alone.

Even in doing wrong and doing evil, a presence and knowing that one is not alone gives some confidence to the individual, how much more when we are doing something good?

We cannot confidently do the work of God if His presence is not with us. We will not be bold enough to say what God wants us to say. Considering the fantastic things God sends people to say, we will lack the boldness to speak His word if He is not with us.

We cannot succeed in the ministry, in preaching, in teaching, in speaking for God, in going where He has sent us and in saying what He has told us if His presence does not go with us. We will be scared and totally confused.

I COULDN'T SPEAK

There was a certain sister causing me a lot of problems in a ministry I was given charge of.

I was a new leader, and she did not believe in me at all. She was not happy with my style of leadership and, surprisingly, she also wouldn't leave to join another group.

One day, The Lord told me to sack her (kick her out). He said to cast her out because she was scorner.

He said, "In your next meeting, sack her."

I decided to confront this sister and sack her. I didn't want to embarrass her or make her feel bad at the meeting, so I waited and called her aside after church. I decided I would give her the boot then, but when the time came, I wasn't bold enough to do it. How could I? She was my friend.

I started stuttering and stammering and going around in circles till she finally asked, "What are you trying to say?"

I was totally confused.

I started suggesting to her to consider focusing on another ministry, then she said, "It's okay, don't count me as part of your people. I don't want to be a part of it anymore." And she turned and walked off.

I was upset and relieved at the same time but then I asked God, why wasn't I able to sack her? And He said to me, "When I told you to do it, you put it off to the time and place you felt was convenient for you."

Instead of doing it when He had said, I was doing my own thing and He wasn't happy with me, so He wasn't with me and although I was doing His work in His name, I lacked the boldness because He wasn't with me. This doesn't mean He had forsaken me, His grace for that just wasn't upon me.

I tell you, if God's presence isn't with you, you will stutter and stammer and make a complete fool of yourself all in the name of "doing His will." The presence of God is essential if you want to do His will and do it confidently.

4. The presence of the Lord makes us important in the eyes of people

> *"And the Lord said unto Joshua, this day will I begin to magnify thee in the sight of all Israel, that they may know that, as I was with Moses, so I will be with thee."*
>
> *-Joshua 3:7*

When God is with someone, He will make them more important. He will make people see them as important. He will make them important to people. People don't listen to us because we are not important.

People don't follow us because they don't see us as anything great. But when God is with us, He will cause people to begin to see us as important. He will make us great in the eyes of people. People will look for us, people will seek our counsel, and people would like to follow us.

People will listen to us, and we will command nations and they will obey. People will begin to respect us, all because God is with us.

When Moses died, he left Joshua in charge. He even announced it in front of the people that God had called Joshua to succeed him.

The truth was nobody would respect a little boy who had been running errands for Moses and pouring water for him to wash his hands when there were mighty men of God that they had seen God transfer Moses's spirit to.

Joshua was scared and trembling, he couldn't preach, he couldn't teach, he couldn't lead the people. He didn't know what to do, and on top of that, they didn't respect him, so they didn't listen to him anyway. But when God's presence came on the scene, He said, "I will magnify you."

In other words, "I will cause them to respect and listen to you. I will make you important. You can't do it on your own; I will sort them out for you."

The presence of God is an extraordinary thing. People don't obey you? Maybe it's because God has not magnified you in their eyes, or it's because God's presence has not yet come on the scene.

When God intervened in Joshua's situation, he became like a

superstar to the point that the people began to mean it when they said, "...We will kill anyone who disobeys you..." (See Joshua 4:14.) The people would only obey him on the condition that God was with him.

OUR DRUMMER BOY

I remember how, a few years ago, I had been told to lead a group of instrumentalists in church. I won't lie, the first few weeks were a nightmare! It was so horrible because nobody would listen to me.

Everybody did what they wanted to, most especially the drummer. He was completely in a world of his own. He did what he wanted, said what he wanted, and came and went as and when he pleased.

There was even a rehearsal we were having that fell on his birthday and so we threw a party for him, bought a cake, drinks, and everything.

Would you believe that out of six or seven of us, he was the only person that didn't turn up? He was out of control, and I had no idea what to do with him.

One night, I got so fed up that I cried out to the Lord. I said to Him, "Father, I can't do this! I'm not called! I'm not a leader! They don't listen to me! I've known these people for a while, and they don't respect me so why would You give them to me to lead them?"

Then something amazing happened, the Lord answered me. He said, "Pray for them. Intercede for each of them."

I prayed all night that night, praying for hours for every one of them. I spent the most hours praying for our drummer. By morning, I felt something break within me and then I heard the Lord say, "Go, I will be with you."

From that day, things turned around totally. Members of the group who hadn't been to church in such a long time started coming. The people started listening to me and even started coming to ask me for help and advice.

For me, the greatest miracle of all was that our drummer actually started to listen to me to the point that another of the leaders in our church said to someone else about me, "she's the only one that can control him, she's the only one he listens to."

People will begin to respect you because of the presence of God with you.

5. The presence of the Lord brings strength and rejuvenation

"Fear thou not; for I am with thee: be not dismayed; for I am thy God: I will strengthen thee; yea, I will help thee; yea, I will uphold thee with the right hand of my righteousness."

-Isaiah 41:10

Samson is the perfect example of this. Samson was a normal man like all his friends, what made the difference was the presence.

When the Spirit of the Lord came upon him, he was strengthened to do all sorts of things, but when the presence of God left Samson, he became weak like anyone else.

(See Judges 15:14-15, Judges 16:18-21.)

Many of God's servants are weak and feeble people like us. The difference is the presence of God. It's the presence of God that strengthens them to withstand the hardships of life in the ministry.

It was the presence of God that strengthened Moses and kept him strong till he died at 120 years of age (Deuteronomy 34:7).

It was the presence of God that strengthened Kathryn Kuhlman to take to the podium and preach and minister in grace and strength even though she was physically ill. The Presence of God brings strength.

> *"but they that wait upon the Lord shall renew their strength; they shall mount up with wings as eagles; they shall run, and not be weary; and they shall walk, and not faint."*
>
> *-Isaiah 40:31*

6. The presence of the Lord brings blessings

To bless means to speak words invoking divine favour. When God is with you, He invokes divine favour on your behalf. He opens doors that no man can shut. He makes a way for you. He draws things and people to you.

God blessed Isaac and the Bible records that he grew mightier than everyone else in the country God told him to reside in. (See Genesis

26:12-16.)

Obed-edom was another person that the Bible clearly records being blessed because of the presence of God.

One day, king David went to recover the ark from captivity and bring it to Jerusalem. As God's people were carrying it, it toppled and someone tried to support it and when he touched it, he died.

David was afraid to bring the Ark to Jerusalem and therefore left it in the house of Obed-edom. (See 2 Samuel 6:9-12.)

When the presence of God is with you, He draws blessings to you. He gives you unmerited favour. He causes things to be well with you. He will cause you to flourish and prosper and increase.

7. The presence of the Lord brings the fullness of joy

> *"Thou wilt shew me the path of life: in thy presence is fullness of joy; at thy right hand there are pleasures for evermore."*
>
> *-Psalms 16:11*

My temperament is very melancholy and that makes me prone to moodiness and depression. More than anything, one battle I must constantly fight is the battle to maintain my joy.

I've fought this battle for many years, and I can confidently say that each time I have come into the presence of the Lord feeling low, depressed, or having a heavy heart, I have not once left without a heart full of joy and singing. I have come to understand that the best way for me to steward my joy is to dwell in the presence of the Lord.

Anytime I sense that I'm losing my joy, no matter where I am, no matter the reason or how I feel, I run to the Lord. I understand that God is my only saving grace, my only source of true joy and I'd rather fall into the hands of God; for great are His mercies.

8. The presence of the Lord destroys obstacles in your path

> *"The mountains quake at him, and the hills melt, and the earth is burned at his presence, yea, the world, and all that dwell therein."*
>
> *-Nahum 1:5*

9. The presence of the Lord brings rest

> *"And he said, My presence shall go with thee, and I will give thee rest."*
>
> *-Exodus 33:14*

For a long time, I did not understand what was meant by "The presence of the Lord will give you rest." I always believed that we were meant to labour till breaking point before stopping for a break, and when we die, then we can get all the rest we need and want.

It wasn't until I started to spend time in the presence of the Lord that I began to understand, one literally comes to a place of rest where nothing in this world can bother or stress them.

I used to be, and still am, a very busy person. Previously, I did all I could to work for the Lord. I was a member of three or four ministries within the church at the same time and was actively present whenever we had an event at church.

I would get stressed to the point that I'd barely make it through that day and then be useless to myself and everyone else for the next week.

Apart from working in church, I was a full-time student at a university in another city, and I also had a part-time job, working at least 20 hours a week in a busy restaurant that I had to travel about two hours to get to.

My life was stressful.

I would get stressed and become frustrated. One night, on my way back from work, I felt the Lord say to me, "Come away. Come away with me."

I was free the next day, so I decided to wait on the Lord that night and the whole of the next day.

I can't describe the rest I felt, the peace that flooded my heart. It was like all the stress just seeped out of my body. Nothing else in the world mattered and even if there had been an earthquake right outside my window, it wouldn't have rattled a hair on my head. I was in a place of total rest.

By the end of the day, I was so refreshed, I felt like I could conquer the world! From that day, I decided to make it a habit to take time off as often as possible to just rest in the presence of the Lord.

Trust me on this one, it's a type of rest that no amount of sleep can give you.

10. The presence of the Lord brings wisdom, knowledge and understanding

See Job 12:9-13.

> *"Now therefore go, and I will be with thy mouth, and teach thee what thou shalt say."*
>
> *-Exodus 4:12*

11. The presence of the Lord brings divine protection, deliverance and salvation

> *"When thou passest through the waters, I will be with thee; and through the rivers, they shall not overflow thee: when thou walkest through the fire, thou shalt not be burned; neither shall the flame kindle upon thee."*
>
> *-Isaiah 43:2*

12. The presence of the Lord gathers people

> *"Fear not: for I am with thee: I will bring thy seed from the east, and gather thee from the west;"*
>
> *-Isaiah 43:5*

As a worker in church, I was given a ministry to build. I was asked to lead a dance group. It was a brilliant idea. I only had two problems with it:

a. I didn't like being around people;
b. I couldn't dance!

My pastor sure had a lot of faith asking me to lead a dance group but, oh well. I had a hard time trying to get people to join the group and to come together to rehearse. It was like a bad dream. So many times, I cried because it was just not working. Then I decided to seek the Lord about it.

I took some time off and spent days praying about it, interceding for the people and asking for wisdom and an anointing to lead. I also asked Him to please teach me how to dance.

After the first day or so, the Lord spoke to me, He said, "Why do you want to dance? Why do you want the people to gather?"

I thought about this carefully and realized that I had no vision for the people. I began to ask the Lord to give me a vision to lead them to, and what He showed me was that it's all for Him.

All we do, whether it's singing, dancing, acting or preaching, it's all for Him and for His glory. We are meant to do what we do to please Him and to glorify Him, so if He wasn't pleased, He wouldn't grace us with His presence.

We had a long conversation and after a few days, my retreat came to an end. The conclusion was that I should seek to please Him, and His presence would be with me.

He told me that when I was doing what He wanted me to do, HE would bring others to join me so that I could lead them and teach them to do the same. I took the time to seek Him, I began to offer my sorry excuse for dancing up to Him. I did it with all my heart.

Whenever I spent time in prayer, I would play worship songs and just dance for Him in His presence. After about a week or so of doing this, I scheduled another rehearsal, and you won't believe that six people turned up!

I did my best to teach them to dance for God as a form of worship, and we grew till our problem became space to rehearse. People would show up for rehearsals and not want to go home afterwards.

Some people who previously wouldn't be caught dead doing anything in church became some of the most faithful members of the group.

From then, I began to understand that the presence of the Lord in and upon my life would draw the people to the ministry. They were not coming to me because of who I was or of what I could do, but because the Lord had decided to grace me with His presence and to draw His people to Himself.

CALLED TO WITNESS

"And we know that all things work together for good to them that love God, to them who are the called according to his purpose."

-Romans 8:28

Without the presence of God, the work of God becomes difficult and tedious. Everyone that has been called by God has been called for a purpose.

There is a reason why God has called you. You are a disciple of Christ, called for a special purpose. That special purpose can be found in Isaiah 43:5-13.

Anyone that has been called by the name of the Lord has been created for the glory of God. Anyone who calls themselves a Christian has been created to be witnesses that the Lord is God.

To be effective witnesses, we must have witnessed something.

To be true witnesses that the Lord is God, we must bring forth our evidence, we must be able to confirm that what is being said is the truth and we can't really do that if we have not witnessed anything.

In Isaiah 43:10, God gives three major components for being an effective witness.

1. That you may know
2. That you may believe
3. That you may understand that He is the Lord and He is the only one that can save

Anyone who has been called by God has been called for Himself.

Every Christian has been called and set aside as separated unto God. Every Christian has been anointed to carry the presence of God.

Every Christian has been anointed for the Kābôd.

Christ never called his followers Christians. In fact, he didn't want followers, he wanted disciples and that's what he called them. It was the people of Antioch that called the believers Christians because they were like the Christ. The disciples were like the anointed one because they spoke and acted like him.

They did the same things he did and bore a good witness of him because the same anointing that was upon him was upon them as well. (See Acts 11:22-26.)

Every Christian has been anointed, set aside for the presence and purpose of God, which is why one is not a Christian if they do not have the Holy Spirit

"But ye are not in the flesh, but in the Spirit, if so be that the Spirit

of God dwell in you. Now if any man have not the Spirit of Christ, he is none of his."

-Romans 8:9

Every Christian has been called to know, believe, and understand that Jesus Christ is Lord of all (he is the only one who saves), and not only to do that but to then bear witness of him. Jesus showed this to us even with the way he handled his disciples, he called them for this very same purpose. (See Mark 3:7-15.)

The best way to get to know who someone really is is to spend time with them. Jesus didn't want his disciples to know him by hearsay, he wanted them to know and believe and truly understand who he was by experience and revelation so that their witness would be a true one.

That was why Jesus asked them in Matthew 16, to see if they actually had a personal revelation of who he was or if they were believing what they heard about him.

When we spend time in the presence of God, we come to know and believe and understand for ourselves who He really is.

The word "revealed" in Matthew 16:17 means "to make information known with an implication that the information can be understood". It is the revelation derived from the Greek, "*Apokalypsis.*"

Peter knew, believed, and now understood that Jesus is indeed the son of God. His disciples had now reached the level of understanding who Jesus really was so one would expect that this should mean that they were to be effective witnesses now, but that wasn't the case.

They now know who Jesus really is and so they should be able to stand boldly and testify and do the works that God has ordained for them to do, but not long after, when Jesus was arrested, in Matthew 26:55-75, the same Peter who had received this revelation denied knowing Jesus three times!

Although Peter knew who Christ really was, he was not able to stand up and bear witness to that fact. This was simply because the presence was gone. He was no longer in the presence of God, so he was not able to. Christ was not with him and so he could not bear witness to who he really was.

Jesus knew this well and that was why he knew Peter would deny him. If Peter and all the other disciples who had been healing the sick and casting out demons and knew that Christ was the son of the living God, were able to forsake him after walking with him for three years, that should tell you how necessary the presence of God is.

Jesus knew that his disciples *needed* his presence to be able to do his father's work and that was why he told them that it was very necessary for him to go and die.

He knew that the only way that God could be with each one of them, no matter where they went, was by the Holy Spirit. (See Matthew 28:18-20, Acts 1:4-5.)

"Nevertheless I tell you the truth; it is expedient for you that I go away: for if I go not away, the Comforter will not come unto you; but if I depart, I will send him unto you."

-John 16:7

THE MINISTRY

When God calls and anoints someone, He does it for a specific reason. Everyone who has been called has a specific calling and a specific task to perform.

Though everyone has been called individually and specifically, there is one theme that cuts across every calling, a common denominator of the call, one primary reason why God uses people.

> *"And I sought for a man among them, that should make up the hedge, and stand in the gap before me for the land, that I should not destroy it: but I found none.*
>
> *Therefore have I poured out mine indignation upon them; I have consumed them with the fire of my wrath: their own way have I recompensed upon their heads, saith the Lord God."*
>
> *-Ezekiel 22:30-31*

Everyone who has been called has been commissioned to stand in the gap before God for the land. Every calling of God has this theme cutting across it. Everyone God has used, He called to make up the hedge, He called to stand in the gap, He called for the sake of the people.

It's Gods hearts cry that His people be saved.

> *"The Lord is not slack concerning his promise, as some men count slackness; but is longsuffering to us - ward, not willing that any should perish, but that all should come to repentance."*
>
> *-2 Peter 3:9*

God doesn't want to destroy the land. He doesn't want to punish the people for their iniquity, but He is a just God, so if someone doesn't bridge the gap and hedge the people, they will definitely be destroyed.

The Bible is saying that God is patiently looking for someone to stand in the gap for His people so that they do not perish. Everyone God has called in any way has had this specific reason as the root of their work.

Everyone called of God has been called to reconcile the people back to God.

It's not about a show of power and might in your ministry. It's about leading the people to God and turning their hearts back to Him. All the works of might, the signs and wonders, the miracles; were in a bid for the people to know who God is and for their hearts to be turned back to Him. (See 2 Corinthians 5:18-19.)

THE HEDGE.

When God made man, He put man in a garden. When man sinned, He was driven out of the garden. For there to have been an "in" and an "out", there must have been a divider. This divider was the hedge that God built around the garden. (See Ezekiel 22:30-31.)

This also is a type of the hedge that God builds around whosoever comes to Him. This hedge is the same hedge that Satan talked about in Job 1:10.

God has put a hedge around all His people. This was a spiritual hedge Satan was talking about because in the natural, there was no hedge around Job.

Jesus also, in John 10, used a similar connotation when he said that he had other sheep he needed to bring into the sheepfold.

A sheepfold is a particular demarcated area that's fenced off by a shepherd for his sheep to dwell safely in. Jesus was talking about a spiritual sheepfold that was protected by a spiritual fence.

The hedge talks about the boundaries God has set for His people to keep them safe. This spiritual boundary is the law of God.

The commandments God has given to His people are not so He can sit on His throne and boss people about; they are for the good of those that believe in Him. (See Deuteronomy 5:29.)

God only wants what's best for His people. Right from Adam, God gave the commandment because He knew that man was sure to go astray if He didn't direct them otherwise.

"All we like sheep have gone astray; we have turned every one to his own way; and the Lord hath laid on him the iniquity of us all."

-Isaiah 53:6

God has always cared about and wanted what's best for His people and that's why even when Adam and Eve disobeyed Him in eating the fruit of the tree of the knowledge of good and evil, His reaction was more that of regret for what they had done than anything else, and that's why He exclaimed, "What have you done?" (See Genesis 3.)

This revealed the gravity of the damage they had inflicted upon themselves due to their disobedience. I don't believe God cursed man because He ate the fruit, I believe that when He told Adam not to eat of the fruit because he would die if he did, God was giving Adam the totality of what would happen.

Adam probably did not understand the effects of having knowledge of good and evil and that's why he did not understand the curses and suffering it would bring. God simply elaborated on the effects and the consequences of their actions when He told them that they and all creation were now cursed. God gives instructions for very good reasons. God knows why He has built the hedge.

The Oxford English Dictionary defines a hedge as a fence or boundary formed by closely growing bushes or shrubs. It is translated from the Hebrew noun *"Gādēr,"* which means "wall, fence, wall made of loose stones from the field without mortar" (Kohlenberger & Swanson).

This hedge is the wall which is also revealed in the book of Nehemiah using the wall of Jerusalem as a type, symbolic of the protective covering God places around His people.

> *"And they said unto me, The remnant that are left of the captivity there in the province are in great affliction and reproach: the wall of Jerusalem also is broken down, and the gates thereof are burned with fire."*
>
> *-Nehemiah 1:3*

God has built this wall around His people. If that wall is broken down, His people suffer reproach and affliction. Jerusalem is the Church and when the walls are broken down, the Church members suffer affliction and reproach.

THE SIGNIFICANCE OF THE WALL

1. The wall is used to protect an area of land *(Job 1:1-10)*

The land is the hearts of the people, and the wall is used to protect the hearts of the people, to keep them safe from external forces and attacks. God is looking for people to make up the hedge to protect His people.

2. The wall is used to divide *(John 10:1,16)*

The wall is what shows the difference between believers and unbelievers. The wall shows boundaries, it is the sheepfold where the sheep are kept in, it is what divides where you can go from where you cannot go.

THE SIGNIFICANCE OF THE DOOR

"Verily, verily, I say unto you, He that entereth not by the door into the sheepfold, but climbeth up some other way, the same is a thief and a robber. But he that entereth in by the door is the shepherd of the sheep. To him the porter openeth; and the sheep hear his voice: and he calleth his own sheep by name, and leadeth them out."

- John 10:1-3

1. The door restricts access

Without a door, anything goes in, and anything goes out. The Bible says guard your heart but without a door, any and everything has access to your heart and that is dangerous because out of the heart flows the issues of life. (See Joshua 6 and Joshua 2:1-7.)

2. The door is the main entrance to the heart

Anything that comes through the window or climbs over a wall is there illegally. However, if they come through the door, they have a legal right to be there because that is the main entrance and access point.

God is a God of principle and legitimacy, and if something is obtained legally, He will not bypass the law.

Everything should be done the right way and if there is no door and demons invade a life, they have a legal right to be there.

MAKE UP THE HEDGE AND STAND IN THE GAP.

"And I sought for a man among them, that should make up the hedge, and stand in the gap before me for the land, that I should not destroy it: but I found none. Therefore have I poured out mine indignation upon them; I have consumed them with the fire of my wrath: their own way have I recompensed upon their heads, saith the Lord God."

-Ezekiel 22:30-31

God is looking for someone to stand in the gap in the hedge. This means that the hedge has been broken.

This implies that the wall, or a part of it has been broken down. God is not looking for who to blame. He is not looking to point fingers. He is not concentrating on who broke the hedge here, His immediate concern is how to bridge the gap and protect the people.

If the hedge is broken, the sheep are in danger. It's not rocket science. It's really simple. As a shepherd, you hedge your sheep into the sheepfold and once that hedge is broken, your sheep are in danger.

It would be a big mistake for you to leave the fence broken and go investigating how it happened. Your priority would be to repair the gap to keep your sheep safe.

That's why Solomon said it was an error that came from the rulers. It was a mistake on the part of the shepherds for the sheep to be bitten. It's a mistake on the part of the rulers for the fence to be left with a gap.

> *"There is an evil which I have seen under the sun, as an error which proceedeth from the ruler: Folly is set in great dignity, and the rich sit in low place. I have seen servants upon horses, and princes walking as servants upon the earth.*
> *He that diggeth a pit shall fall into it; and whoso breaketh an hedge, a serpent shall bite him."*
>
> —Ecclesiastes 10:5-8

It is a mistake that Jesus as the good shepherd would not make and that's why God was happy with him. He'd do anything to keep the sheep safe.

(See John 10:1-12.)

As you can see, this is the cry of God's heart as a good ruler and that is why He looks for someone to stand in the gap.

Yes, there are consequences for every action, but God is not so much concerned about laying blame as He is about fixing the problem, seeing as the hedge is the commandment of God and breaking the hedge is equivalent to disobeying His commandments.

Knowing this, then understand that to "make up the hedge" is an action translated from the Hebrew verb "*Gādar*" meaning to:

1. Build a stone wall
2. Heap up stones for a wall

BUILDING THE WALL

> *"And I sought for a man among them, that should make up the hedge, and stand in the gap before me for the land, that I should not destroy it: ..."*
>
> -Ezekiel 22:30

1. It is the will of God that we build the wall

God is the one looking for a man to bridge the gap. It's the will of God that His people be saved and delivered and kept.

No matter who He chooses, we must first understand that it is ultimately God who is trying to save His people.

It is easy to emphasize more on the person who is making up the hedge and protecting you from being hurt, but we must understand that it is God who is actually trying to protect us. It is God who sends whoever has come and it is God who is making up the hedge, He is using a man.

Understand that it's the will of God to keep His people safe. He is a kind and caring God. Even when, due to His nature as a just God, His people should be consumed with fire and their own ways recompensed upon their own heads, He would go out of His way and do all He can to save His people, preferring mercy to than judgement.

> *"For I desired mercy, and not sacrifice; and the knowledge of God more than burnt offerings."*
>
> -Hosea 6:6

2. God is looking for a man

God is not looking for angels or animals to bridge the gap. He is not looking for cherubim or any celestial beings; he is looking for a man (generic).

The first and foremost qualification of anyone who is to make up the hedge or stand in the gap is that he must be man. Not a man as in a male, a man as in a human being. God is not looking for two men or a company of people; He is looking for just one person at a time.

God needed someone as a go-between to be his hands and feet, to make up the vast difference between the people and himself. That is why we have Ministers of God. They bridge the gap between people and God. They are men but are sent by and speak for God. (See Exodus 3:1-10.)

He needs only one person. It's singular. God is looking for a man so if you have a group or company mindset, you disqualify yourself. If you are not an individual who is able to make up your mind, and rather have a flow-with-the-crowd mentality, you disqualify yourself. God is looking for one man.

God may call many people to do the same thing but the call of God is an individual thing and if you are not convinced and fully persuaded that this is what God has called you to do, whether people agree and support you or not, you will not be able to do the work of God.

3. God is looking for someone among them

Whatever group you are in, God is looking for one person in that group to stand in the gap for them. God will not call you to stand in the gap for a group you don't belong to. God was looking for a man among, not above, not below, but among the people.

When God was looking for someone to deliver His people from Egypt, He called someone who was one of them. He called Moses who was also an Israelite.

God needed a man to bridge the gap between Him as a Spirit and the children of Israel as humans. God called Nehemiah to build the wall of Jerusalem and to stand in the gap for his people because he was one of them. (Nehemiah 1:1-4, 2:1-5.)

Repeatedly, you see God calling and using someone from among the people to save them. He used Esther to save her people; He used David to save his people. Christ was sent to preach to the Jews. Christ came unto his own people. (See John 1:12.)

When God wants to save a group of people, He will always raise up someone from among those people to stand in the gap.

What group are you in? Could it be that God will find you to stand in the gap for your family, your tribe, your nation, your church, or even just your ministry?

4. It is a call to stand before Him

God is looking for someone to stand before Him, someone to present themselves before Him, someone whose assigned position is before Him.

To stand before God simply means to stand in His presence.

Not everyone has permission to come into the presence of a king. It takes a matter or a person of great importance to be able to get an audience with the king.

Not everyone can present themselves before a king so when God calls someone and gives them permission to stand in His presence, it's a great honour.

When the king assigns you a position in his courts, it's a great honour and a great promotion. It means you work for, live in and all your needs are provided for by the royal household. You have access to his presence, and you have the privilege of presenting whatever case you have before him, and even sometimes, the privilege to influence his judgment on certain matters.

The call to stand is the call to serve Him. It is the call to minister unto Him.

> *"My sons, be not now negligent: for the Lord hath chosen you to stand before him, to serve him, and that ye should minister unto*

him, and burn incense."

-2 Chronicles 29:11

To serve is to perform duties or services for another person or organisation. It means to be of use in satisfying a specific purpose, and the thing to understand is whom you are serving.

Although we are building the wall to save the people, we are not building the wall for them, we are doing it for God. The shepherd will never ask his sheep how they want him to build the hedge around them, he just gets on with the job. In the same way, when God calls us to build the wall and bridge the gap, we get our building plans and instructions from Him and not them.

We are building for Him. We are serving Him. How people respond to us, or whether they receive us or not, is not our problem.

In the end, it's God whom we are answerable to. The call is from God, it's about Him, not us, not the people; Him.

5. It is to save the land from destruction

God is looking for someone who will present themselves before Him for a specific reason; People who will come into His presence for a specific purpose and boldly plead their cause.

Queen Esther is a person in the Bible who can be used to explain this. When her people were in danger of destruction, she presented herself before the king to present their case before him, when no one was authorized to do so.

Firstly, she had not been summoned and to come before the king without being summoned was punishable by death. Secondly, she was a Jew and the law that had been passed was to kill all the Jews.

The king could have said she be the first to die as an example to the people that the law must be obeyed. She was ready to die, knowing that she tried her best and she gave her all to save her people for it was what she had been called to do. (See Esther 4, 7, and 8.)

Esther was able to influence the king's judgment, not by removing the law that had already been passed but by the king passing a law that enabled her people to protect themselves, a law of mercy to overrule the law of judgment.

She came boldly, presenting herself before the king. She put her life on the line for the people. She was afraid for herself but stood in the gap for her people, she was not afraid to receive the full force of the enemy's blow to the gap. She knew she could easily be killed, but she trusted God and stood for her people.

God used Esther to stand in the gap for Israel.

HOW TO BUILD THE WALL

The Bible gives accounts of different people who achieved many different things. One of the people it talks about is Nehemiah, an Israelite, who re-built the wall of Jerusalem. (See Nehemiah 1 and 2.)

He is a good example, as he was successfully able—with God's help, to build the wall of Jerusalem and, make up the hedge and stand in the gap before God, for the land, to save it from destruction.

We must learn one great lesson on from him.

LESSON ONE

BEGINNING BEFORE GOD:

The foundation of fasting and prayer

When we begin in the presence of the Lord, we position ourselves to hear from Him and to receive His plans. We must always remember that, as much as God calls people to do this work, it is His work and, in the end, He is the only one that can do it and do it the way it should be done.

Nehemiah began before God

Nehemiah was moved to fast and pray for his people. He didn't just cry.

> *"And it came to pass, when I heard these words, that I sat down and wept, and mourned certain days, and fasted, and prayed before the God of heaven,"*
>
> *-Nehemiah 1:4*

He was so moved by the condition of his people that he wept and cried and mourned, but after doing that, he got up and fasted and prayed to God. It's not enough to just feel it, you need to do something about the state of others.

Esther began before God

Not just Nehemiah, but everyone who was called as a deliverer in the Bible began with fasting and prayer.

Before Esther presented herself before the King to deliver her people, she fasted and prayed.

> *"Then Esther bade them return Mordecai this answer, Go, gather together all the Jews that are present in Shushan, and fast ye for me, and neither eat nor drink three days, night or day: I also and my maidens will fast likewise; and so will I go in unto the king, which is not according to the law: and if I perish, I perish."*
>
> *-Esther 4:15-16*

Jesus began before God

Before Jesus began his ministry, he was led into the wilderness where he fasted and prayed for 40 days and nights.

> *"Then was Jesus led up of the Spirit into the wilderness to be tempted of the devil. And when he had fasted forty days and forty nights, he was afterward an hungred."*
>
> *-Matthew 4:1-2*

Moses began before God

Moses, God's chosen leader, whom He sent to deliver the children of Israel prayed and fasted twice for 40 days and nights. It was not stated in the Bible that he fasted and prayed before he went to Egypt to stand before Pharaoh, but we see him fasting and praying to pacify God's anger against the children of Israel.

> "And Moses went into the midst of the cloud, and gat him up into the mount: and Moses was in the mount forty days and forty nights... And he was there with the Lord forty days and forty nights; he did neither eat bread, nor drink water. And he wrote upon the tablets the words of the covenant, the Ten Commandments."
>
> -Exodus 24:18, Exodus 34:28

★★★

God works through people as vessels. For Him to do so, the people have to work with Him by yielding themselves to Him.

We are all vessels in the hand of the Lord and so, to do what He wants us to do, we need to be totally yielded to Him. We need to remain in sync with Him so that we don't mess things up.

When we spend time fasting and praying in the presence of God, just like Moses did, He gives us the step-by-step plan He has for us to build, and His presence is also with us.

If God has called you and placed in your heart to build a wall or hedge, you must spend time in His presence, waiting on Him for the directions, instructions, and the grace you need to do so.

WHY CHRISTIANS GO TO CHURCH

PART ONE:
THE CHURCH

BASIC CHRISTIANITY

In order to understand the Church and the significant role it plays in the lives of Christians, we must first understand Christianity.

The basics of Christianity have been dealt with in previous chapters, most specifically, in the section *Understanding Christianity*.

Being a Christian is having an intimate relationship with Christ that influences your thoughts, actions, and intentions till they become identical to his. At this point, others look at you and see Christ.

Christianity is founded on our reconciliation with God through the sacrifice Jesus made for us.

It is also true the cares of life and the deceitfulness of riches can turn our focus away from seeking Christ. Therefore, I will not neglect the truth that some who have become born again do sometimes grow distant from God.

In these cases, we only need to acknowledge we have sinned, and turn back to God in repentance.

UNDERSTANDING THE CHURCH

Some refer to the Church as the body of Christ, while others may refer to it as a religious house of worship. But the word "Church" was first used in the Bible by Jesus himself not long before he was crucified. This was when he mentioned to Peter that he would build it.

> "He saith unto them, But whom say ye that I am? And Simon Peter answered and said, Thou art the Christ, the Son of the living God. And Jesus answered and said unto him, Blessed art thou, Simon Barjona: for flesh and blood hath not revealed it unto thee, but my Father which is in heaven. And I say also unto thee, That thou art Peter, and upon this rock I will build my church; and the gates of hell shall not prevail against it. And I will give unto thee the keys of the kingdom of heaven: and whatsoever thou shalt bind on earth shall be bound in heaven: and whatsoever thou shalt loose on earth shall be loosed in heaven."
>
> - Matthew 16:15-19

Translated from the Greek word "*Ekklēsian*," the noun, *Church*, speaks of an assembly or religious congregation. Jesus told Peter he will build a religious congregation the gates of hell shall not prevail against, an assembly that will not be swallowed up by hell.

An assembly speaks of a group of people gathered in a place for a common purpose. A congregation is a gathering or collection of people. The Church Jesus is building, is a group, gathering, or collection of people with the common purpose of withstanding the gates of hell based on the revelation that Jesus Christ is the son of God.

The Church is not one person, it is a group, a collection of at least two or three people, who Jesus gives the keys to the Kingdom of heaven and the authority to bind and loose things in heaven and on earth. (See Matthew 18:15-20.)

Jesus led people to gather, with a promise to be in their midst when they did so on his account. These people who are congregated or assembled in his name are what he refers to as his Church.

We can therefore conclude that a Church is an assembled body of Christians. Without the assembly, there is no Church.

When the disciples first began gathering, they did so in each other's homes. As they grew in number, they needed a bigger space to meet. The church buildings of today solve the problem of a meeting place big enough to contain the assembly, making it important for believers to then come the church (the building) to be a part of the Church (the Assembly).

JEWS AND CHRISTIANS

After the flood that washed the world clean, Noah and his household spread to repopulate humanity on earth. But as the population increased, evil multiplied, and people withdrew from God.

One of the descendants of Noah along the line of Shem (Noah's first son) was a man named Terah. Terah had three sons: Nahor, Haran and Abram (who later became Abraham).

After Haran passed, Terah was struck with grief and eventually passed also, leaving Abram to take care of Haran's son, Lot.

Now, God spoke to Abram, instructing him to leave where he was settled and head off to a land God would show him. God also promised to make his name great, and to make of him a great nation.

This became what we know as the nation of Israel.

Abraham had two sons, the younger of whom was called Isaac, the child of promise. Isaac went on to have twins, the younger being Jacob (whose name was changed to Israel).

Israel had twelve sons, and he shamelessly picked a favourite: Joseph. Israel's unapologetic favouritism of Joseph, and (as though that wasn't bad enough) Joseph's propensity for snitching—and sharing his dreams about his family bowing to him—inspired hatred among Israel's other children. Naturally, they eventually got fed up with Joseph and decided to get rid of him.

Lucky for him, they reconsidered their plans of fratricide, deciding to make him good for something by selling him and only faking his death. So, off Joseph went with a group of passing traders on their way to Egypt, where he was sold as a slave to an influential Egyptian named Potiphar.

Over time, Potiphar was impressed enough by Joseph to promote him to be his second. But Potiphar, it seems, was not the only one impressed. Potiphar's wife took an interest in Joseph, and when he refused her advances, she accused him of attempted rape.

Joseph, the immigrant-slave-turned-aide-de-camp, became a convict. And because Potiphar was a cut above the rest, so was the prison he left Joseph to rot in.

In jail, Joseph the Dreamer became chums with his two cellmates, interpreting their dreams. This friendship eventually led to a job recommendation to interpret Pharaoh's dreams warning about a coming famine. His success in this got him both his freedom and a great job as Pharaoh's second.

During the terrible famine, Israel and his family relocated to Goshen, in Egypt (on Joseph's tab), where they and their descendants remained even after the famine. The descendants of Israel grew in number until a Pharaoh who did not know the histories began to oppress them.

In their oppression, they cried out to the Lord, and He sent them a deliverer, Moses.

Moses led the children of Israel out of Egypt with many signs and wonders, to the glory of God, taking them across the Red Sea and through the wilderness to the foot of the promised land. During the 40 years journey, the Lord taught the Israelites through Moses to be different from the nations around them, to get rid of their pagan cultures, idol worship, and to worship the one, true God. These teachings are what formed the basis of their culture and religious practices.

One of the things Moses did teach them was that God would reconcile them to Himself by another prophet like him whom God would raise. This prophet was the promised Messiah that the Jews waited for.

That Messiah is Jesus.

Jesus Christ came, raised from among them just like Moses, fulfilling this scripture, meaning that Jesus was a Jew. Jesus practised the Jewish customs and traditions because those were handed down by God through Moses.

Where Christianity differs from Judaism is that, after the resurrection of Jesus, some of the Jews believed that Jesus was the promised Messiah while some didn't, although they did believe he was a prophet. All those who believed that Jesus was the promised Messiah also began to spread this good news to the world as instructed by him, praising God and sharing his teachings.

These believers in Jesus were persecuted and killed—most especially by one Saul—spreading the gospel further as they fled from Jerusalem.

After his conversion, Saul changed his name to Paul and preached the gospel of Jesus Christ with zeal and great conviction, leading many to the knowledge of God through Christ, and teaching them to change their ways. As these believers met and worshipped, being changed and conformed to the image of Christ, the name "Christian" was coined in Antioch.

Thus, Christianity became a separate religious movement to Judaism.

SEVEN REASONS WHY THE CHURCH IS IMPORTANT

1. The Church is Jesus's building project

> "And I say also unto thee, That thou art Peter, and upon this rock I will build my church; and the gates of hell shall not prevail against it."
>
> - Matthew 16:18

Jesus is building his Church, and everything he does is important. Therefore, the existence of the Church is important.

2. The Church has been given the keys to the Kingdom of Heaven

> "And if he shall neglect to hear them, tell it unto the church: but if he neglect to hear the church, let him be unto thee as an heathen man and a publican. Verily I say unto you, whatsoever ye shall bind on earth shall be bound in heaven: and whatsoever ye shall loose on earth shall be loosed in heaven."
>
> - Matthew 18:17-18

Jesus has given the keys of the kingdom to his Church, and this means that the Church has the power to lock and unlock things in the spiritual realm. The Church, as a body, has been given the authority to open and close certain things that individual Christians would have no power to.

3. Jesus has promised to be wherever the Church gathers

> *"For where two or three are gathered together in my name, there am I in the midst of them."*
>
> *- Matthew 18:20*

As Christians, the most important relationship we can have is with God, through Jesus. Here, Jesus guarantees he will be found where his people are gathered. This is sort of an X-marks-the-spot for all those seeking him.

4. The Church is the body of Christ

> *"And hath put all things under his feet, and gave him to be the head over all things to the church, which is his body, the fulness of him that filleth all in all."*
>
> *- Ephesians 1:22-23*

Jesus is the most important person to have ever walked the earth, and his spiritual body is the Church. This makes the Church the most important spiritual body to ever be on earth.

When God moves on earth, He does so through the Church of Jesus Christ. God makes Himself manifest to believers and nonbelievers alike, but only through the Church does He reconcile humanity back to Himself.

5. Christ is the head of the Church

> *"And he is the head of the body, the church: who is the beginning, the firstborn from the dead; that in all things he might have the preeminence."*
>
> *- Colossians 1:18*

The spiritual head, as an authority figure, speaks of a spiritual covering, among other things. It is the protection provided by someone more powerful, influential, or authoritative.

In certain places one may find that people are provided protection by those they submit to, and retribution is taken by the authority when one of theirs is wronged.

This same analogy applies with Christ and the Church. Anyone who is in the Church is under Christ's covering, and seeing as Christ has been given all power and authority both in heaven and on earth, he's the best covering to have over your life.

6. Christ loves the Church

> *"Husbands, love your wives, even as Christ also loved the church, and gave himself for it;"*
>
> *- Ephesians 5:25*

Jesus loved the world enough to die for it and freely offers whatsoever is needed to live a godly life. As people turn to God and gather together, the Church is established as a chosen people whom God loves. (See John 3:16-17.)

7. Christ sends his angel to speak to the Churches

"I Jesus have sent mine angel to testify unto you these things in the churches. I am the root and the offspring of David, and the bright and morning star."

- Revelation 22:16

Apart from Jesus visiting the Churches himself, he also sends his angel with messages to them. Jesus uses the gathering almost as an Embassy for heavenly activity on earth.

10 THINGS THAT HAPPEN IN THE CHURCH

1. Baptism

In Acts 2, Baptism was one instruction Jesus gave his disciples before he left the earth. He instructed them to baptise in the name of the Father, the Son and the Holy Ghost.

Baptism is immersion in water. This was what John did in the Jordan to prepare the way for Jesus. He preached the baptism of repentance and immersed people in the river Jordan.

This is an act, signifying a spiritual death and rebirth, being immersed and resurrected anew as you come up, dead to sin and alive to Christ.

> *"I indeed baptize you with water unto repentance: but he that cometh after me is mightier than I, whose shoes I am not worthy to bear: he shall baptize you with the Holy Ghost, and with fire:"*
>
> *- Matthew 3:11*

2. Salvation

Only in the Church of God can you be sure that the offer of salvation will be made. With every altar call, as the Word of God is preached, an invitation to accept Jesus as the Messiah and to be saved from the damnation of hell is made.

The role of the Church on earth is to reconcile the world to God, and this is done by freely offering the great gift of salvation to all.

3. Teaching

Everyone has a mindset—things they believe and have set as truths in their minds. These things may not necessarily be correct, or even true, but people will never know some things until they are taught them.

A lot of people act out of ignorance. They would probably not behave or react the way they do if they knew better. The problem is no one is teaching them better.

> *"Go ye therefore, and teach all nations, baptizing them in the name of the Father, and of the Son, and of the Holy Ghost: teaching them to observe all things whatsoever I have commanded you: and, lo, I am with you alway, even unto the end of the world. Amen."*
>
> *- Matthew 28:19-20*

Jesus instructed his disciples to teach new converts and believers the things that he had taught them. This is why the breaking down of the Word of God, especially the words of Jesus, into bite-size nuggets of wisdom for easy comprehension is very important.

Anyone who misses Church gatherings actually exempts themselves from the teachings on how to live a righteous and godly life in these last days. Thus, they will most likely struggle and eventually fail in their Christian walk, as they will be trying to pass tests on topics they have never come across or been taught before simply because they skipped lessons.

4. Fellowship

A synonym for fellowship, which will help convey this better, is friendship.

Anyone who hopes to walk the straight and narrow needs to surround themselves with likeminded people who will celebrate, encourage, understand, and communicate with them on a spiritual level as well as a social one.

If one was lacking in such areas of friendship, when they experience a great victory in their Christian walk, how do they celebrate such joy with another who shrugs off their accomplishment as unpopular behaviour in obedience to an outdated law? And how can they expect to get godly advice or encouragement in their low moments if they do not have a friend well equipped to give it?

Godly friends also go a long way towards helping one become stable in a Church. It is very difficult to leave a place you are loved and belong to, no matter what you experience. But it is easy to be displaced from somewhere you only visit once in a while and at your own convenience.

5. Breaking of bread

Bonds are formed over food. Even those who don't like food bond over the fact that they don't like food.

The breaking of bread not only signifies the Lord's supper which he asked his disciples to repeat in memory of him, it also signifies the sharing of one's source of sustenance.

Food and water are the body's source of vitality, and in communion with one another, we break bread, sharing the very basic source of sustenance we have. By this, we say to each other, "You are important to me, I need you to survive."

A barbeque, lunch, breakfast, dinner or even tea and biscuits shared during fellowship, offers the chance for believers to bond, let down their walls and build bridges of friendships that will last a lifetime.

6. Prayers

The Church is a spiritual organism whose life force is prayer. Prayer is simply communion with God, and seeing as the Church belongs to and is run by God, nothing can be done (or done right) without communion with Him.

Therefore, everything must be done by prayer, and nothing done without it. Both collective and individual, the public and the private, the personal and the communal prayers are important for the proper functioning of the Church as a whole.

7. Signs and wonders

There are certain signs that Jesus said would follow those who believe in him. These signs are not spiritual fireworks given to us to entertain the masses. These are signs to prove to the world that God is real, and that Jesus is the way, the truth, and the life.

A chesty cough, wheezing and a fever are all signs present when a person has a chest infection, bronchitis, lung cancer or pneumonia. These signs make one aware of the presence of something that is not normally there, allowing them to search for the cause of these anomalies.

So also, when people see the signs and wonders, it makes them aware of the presence of something in the life of the believer that is not normal, or naturally occurring, in the human experience. It causes them to realize the presence of an external being, one greater than them, thus stirring in them the interest in and the desire to know God for themselves.

Signs and wonders are not toys; they are tools for the salvation of others.

8. Giving

Giving in church is not limited to the church institution and to finances alone. Volunteering of one's time, gifts, abilities, and services to the Church and each other is also giving.

The Church is not a business and therefore does not generate an income, but it still must be maintained and run for our benefit and that of mankind at large.

Seeing as we live in a financially driven world, it is not feasible to run the Church without money. There are bills to pay, things to get, and people to serve. A Church that meets on a particular premises, is responsible for covering the costs generated by using the facilities made available.

This is why voluntary service in the Church is also crucial to the running of it. If we all gave our time and gifts freely, the running cost of the church would reduce significantly, allowing us to do more and reach more people.

These days, believers need to be encouraged and stirred up to put something towards the house of God that is blessing them. They almost need to be bribed with blessings from the Word of God before they pay their tithe or give an offering.

It is the way of children to not be responsible enough to maintain the things that sustain them. So also, it is with new Christians to not be responsible enough to maintain the Church that sustains them without being promised great riches and blessings in return.

I would encourage you as a Christian to give to the work and the house of God. If you build a house for God, He will surely build a home for you. If you take an interest in the things of God, the same God that created the universe, who set the planets in motion and the stars in their place, that same God who holds the waters of the earth in the palm of His hand, will take an interest in you.

9. Daily meetings

The believers did everything together, thus making it easier for them to gather every day. In today's fast-paced society, it becomes more of a challenge to meet with other Christians on a regular basis. It is, however, not impossible.

For some, we work, go to school or even live with other believers and so we interact with them every day. We are strengthened by one another and build stronger bonds with each other. For others, that opportunity has not been afforded. This just means that, where possible, one may need to make the extra effort to meet with other believers. Even if it is just for service and fellowship afterwards.

You would meet up with your friends for dinner, bowling, to go to the movies or just to watch Netflix and hang out. These would not be structured, formal settings. So also, the Church gathering does not need to be in a structured, formal setting.

Remember that the Church is the gathering of those who believe in the name of Jesus. And whenever believers gather, the Word of God will always, at some point or another, be shared.

10. Praising God

The common denominator between Christians is the belief in God and reconciliation to Him through Jesus Christ. Apart from this one great gift of salvation, there are numerous other things that God has done in our lives, individually and collectively, and it is only natural to acknowledge Him for these.

That simple acknowledgement is praise in its most basic form. Praising God is making mention of, and giving thanks for, the things He has done. We worship God by reverencing who He is, and we praise Him by acknowledging what He has done.

This is done when we assemble as saints in the name of Christ.

CHURCH MEMBERSHIP

"God decided in advance to adopt us into his own family by bringing us to himself through Jesus Christ. This is what he wanted to do, and it gave him great pleasure."

- Ephesians 1:5 (New Living Translation)

When a person becomes born again, they become adopted into a new family. This family is the Church.

There is truth in saying that there are many churches, and people can choose where they want to go. However, the Lord directs people to where He wants them to be, and when they get there, He wants them to remain planted so they can grow.

THE LORD DIRECTED ME TO MY CHURCH

In college, I attended services at the Catholic Church. I was a faithful member, and I enjoyed the homilies given by some of the priests because I understood what they were teaching me. But there was always this nagging feeling in me that there was more.

I wanted more.

Now, anyone who knows anything about the Catholic Church will understand that it is a very good Church, very disciplined in every way, and also very deep in their knowledge of the Word of God. I, however, didn't seem to grasp any of it. I quickly got bored of the routine, and one day, I prayed, telling God, "There has to be more to You than this."

I asked Him to manifest and reveal Himself to me. Not long after that, I found myself visiting a church service at a very charismatic church—the kind of church I had sworn I would not be caught dead in. In fact, I used to make fun of such churches for their extravagance. I thought they were loud, excessive, and flighty.

I remember being in the service and, although it was much longer and more uncomfortable than I was used to, I just knew that the Lord was there, and it was where he wanted me to be.

★★★

Being a member of a church for a long time comes with its fair share of issues, and heartaches as well as joys and successes. So, when issues arise, you don't just leave the church, just like in a family, because you're having a rough day or not getting along with your siblings, that doesn't mean you move out, change your name, and disown the family.

Being a member of a church means you are faithful to that gathering, and not just any you feel like on any given day. The Bible describes the Church as a body and the people as its members. Just imagine if your fingernail decided, "Today, it looks like I'm closer to the hip, I'm just going to lodge myself in the hip for the time being." Imagine the kind of pain you will be in, losing a fingernail and then having one lodged in your hip.

This is the kind of damage we do to the body of Christ when we constantly shift from church to church, not being stable enough in one place to help build the Church.

God leads us to the best place for us to be in His body, and He expects us to stay there.

THREE REWARDS OF BEING A STABLE CHURCH MEMBER

1. You will flourish if you are stable

> *"Those that be planted in the house of the Lord shall flourish in the courts of our God."*
>
> *- Psalm 92:13*

The Bible promises flourishing to those who are planted in the house of the Lord. This means, having deep roots in the house of God such that you cannot easily be moved. This will result in you thriving, blooming, prospering, and becoming successful.

2. You will have a family to celebrate your victories and mourn losses with if you are stable

> *"Rejoice with them that do rejoice, and weep with them that weep."*
>
> *- Romans 12:15*

The Church of God is a family, and when you decide to be a part of that family, you will be surrounded by believers to celebrate victories with. You will also have a great family of people to be with you in times of mourning, loss, or when you are going through challenges.

One very difficult thing to experience is being surrounded by people and still feeling alone. When you decide to be stable and committed to God and to His Church, you start to invest freely. You don't hold yourself back, and you begin to develop deeper and better relationships with those around you.

These are the family members who will stick with you when you need a shoulder to cry on or a hand to hold, and will celebrate with you when you need a friend to be happy with and for you.

3. You will see the fruit of your labour if you are stable

A farmer who keeps replanting their crops every week or two will not reap anything from what they have planted. So also, the Christian who hops from gathering to gathering has no real roots anywhere and therefore cannot expect to bear any sort of fruit *(James 1:6-8)*.

What is the point of labouring to be a Christian and not having a reward for it? What is the use of all your hard work if it will come to naught? What is the use of investing in your Christian life and then it amounts to nothing?

Therefore, it is a blessing to be stable, committed to the assembly the Lord leads you to. Because, when you are planted in one place and are stable, you are able to grow, to invest, and to receive freely. You can see the effects of the Word of God in your life, and you are able to reap the harvest of the seeds you've sown.

I remember, when I was still a new believer, the Holy Spirit spoke to me about being stable and committed to the church I was in. He explained to me that if I came to God, praying and crying for something, and God decided to answer my prayer, He would send His angels to deliver the blessing to the one place He is sure I will come to meet Him every week (church).

How sad it would be if, on the day my answer came, I decided to go to another church for that Sunday.

That revelation stayed with me till this day. It may not be the best analogy, and God definitely can and will meet us where we are, but a deep truth was revealed to me through it: God expects to meet us at a particular place, just as He called Moses, Jesus, and others in the Bible to come away to specific places to be with Him.

During these divine appointments, God sends His angels to specific locations with our blessings and the answer to our prayers, but if we do not meet them at the appointed time and place, we often miss out on what God planned for us.

DIFFERENT CHURCHES, DIFFERENT DOCTRINES

"Jesus replied, 'If I want him to remain alive until I return, what is that to you? As for you, follow me...'"

- John 21:22 (New Living Translation)

It is true that there are many different churches, and people often ask, "If it is all one body, why are the different churches preaching different things?"

The reason for this is, just as the different parts of the body have different functions, so also, the different churches have different functions. The message of the Church as a whole remains the same: salvation through Jesus Christ. But the emphasis of each church differs depending on its commission.

In the same way Peter queries what will happen to John and Jesus basically tells him to mind his own business, Jesus has given every church and every ministry an emphasis and tells them to *mind their own business* when they start querying another church's doctrines.

"Then they that gladly received his word were baptized: and the

> *same day there were added unto them about three thousand souls. And they continued steadfastly in the apostles' doctrine and fellowship, and in breaking of bread, and in prayers."*
>
> *- Acts 2:41-42*

It is important for churches to follow in their own Apostles' doctrines and not get carried away, chasing after everything that they see and hear. In the book of Revelation, each church was sent a different message, depending on what the Lord needed them to focus on. This would have been the church's emphasis at the time, and it would have been up to the leader or Apostle of that church to emphasize it. This is why the letters were sent to the angels of the churches, and not the whole congregation.

1. The Ephesus Church would have needed to emphasize love

> *"Write this letter to the angel of the church in Ephesus... I have seen your hard work and your patient endurance... you have patiently suffered for me without quitting. But I have this complaint against you. You don't love me or each other as you did at first... turn back to me and do the works you did at first..."*
>
> *- Revelation 2:1-5 (New Living Translation)*

Under these given circumstances, the Apostle of the church in Ephesus would likely then lay more emphasis on loving God and loving each other. Fledgling gatherings that received this message and emphasis may then run with it, resulting in new ministries called things like "Agape Church," or "The Love of God International Ministries, Ephesus Branch."

2. The Smyrna Church would have needed to emphasize faithfulness unto death

> *"Write this letter to the angel of the church in Smyrna... I know about your suffering and poverty... I know the blasphemy of those opposing you... Don't be afraid of what you are about to suffer... if you remain faithful even when facing death, I will give you the crown of life."*
>
> *- Revelation 2:8-10 (New Living Translation)*

At the time, the church in Smyrna was facing grave persecution, and some of them were to be killed for the sake of Christ. Jesus knew this, and he told John to write to the church to lay emphasis on being faithful through the persecution they were facing.

This message of faithfulness and perseverance through suffering would have become the emphasis of the church at the time.

3. The Pergamum Church would have needed to emphasize radical Christian living among unbelievers and intolerance of false doctrines

> *"Write this letter to the angel of the church in Pergamum... I know you live in a city where Satan has his throne... I have a few complaints against you. You tolerate some among you whose*

teaching is like that of Balaam... in a similar way, you have some Nicolatians among you who follow the same teaching. Repent of your sin..."

- Revelation 2:12-16 (New Living Translation)

The congregation in Pergamum were living where Satan himself was and he was attacking them with false teachings and false doctrines which were making them complacent and tolerant of things they ought not to tolerate. At this point, Jesus sent a letter to the church leadership to say, "Fix up and get radical or you won't survive the attack."

On receiving this message, these leaders would have then laid emphasis on this teaching, establishing in the hearts of the congregation to be radical.

The members of that church would probably not have needed that doctrine if they had changed locations and moved to Ephesus because the necessity of that teaching was generated by the attack they were experiencing, due to their church being located where Satan was.

4. The Thyatira Church would have had to emphasize purity

"Write this letter to the angel of the church in Thyatira... I can see your constant improvement in all things. But I have this complaint against you. You are permitting that woman – that Jezebel who calls herself a prophet – to lead my servants astray. She teaches them to commit sexual sin and to eat food offered to idols... she does

not want to turn away from her immorality... those who commit adultery with her will suffer greatly unless they repent and turn away from their evil deeds... I also have a message for the rest of you in Thyatira who have not followed this false teaching... I will ask nothing more of you except that you hold tightly to what you have until I come."

- Revelation 2:18-25 (New Living Translation)

When the leader of a congregation receives such a message from Jesus, they would focus their emphasis on repenting of adultery, immorality, sexual sins, and idolatry. Because there are those the message doesn't apply to, that would not stop the Apostle from emphasizing it in their teachings to *immunize* the unaffected while treating the affected.

5. The Sardis Church would have had to emphasize revival

"Write this letter to the angel of the church in Sardis... I know all the things you do, and that you have a reputation for being alive – but you are dead. Wake up! Strengthen what little remains, for even what is left is almost dead... Go back to what you heard and believed at first; hold to it firmly... yet there are some in the church in Sardis who have not soiled their clothes with evil..."

- Revelation 3:1-4 (New Living Translation)

Again, we see a church where the message only seems to apply to some of the congregation. In this situation, the church looked like a good, healthy, and thriving church. But Jesus said they were asleep, dead and needing to be stirred and shaken.

This church needed a revival, and that is what the leader would have needed to emphasize until the people had repented and turned back to what they first believed.

6. The Philadelphia Church would have had to emphasize victory

> *"Write this letter to the angel of the church in Philadelphia... I have opened a door for you that no one can close. You have little strength, yet you obeyed my word and did not deny me. Look, I will force those who belong to Satan's synagogue... to come and bow down at your feet. They will acknowledge that you are the ones I love... I will protect you from the great time of testing... Hold on to what you have so that no one will take away your crown."*
>
> *- Revelation 3:7-11 (New Living Translation)*

Imagine the adulterous members of the church in Thyatira streaming in live to watch the Philly pastor preaching about being the head and not the tail, declaring to his congregation that God will reward them, and to hold on and keep on doing what they are doing. They would be listening to the word of God, a direct message from Jesus himself, but not the right word for them.

7. The Church in Laodicea would have had to emphasize a

burning passion or fire

> "Write this letter to the angel of the church in Laodicea... you are neither hot nor cold. I wish you were one or the other'... You say, 'I am rich. I have everything I want, I don't need a thing!' ... I advise you to buy gold from me–gold that has been purified by fire...also buy white garments from me so you will not be shamed by your nakedness, and ointment for your eyes So you will be able to see... turn from your indifference."
>
> - Revelation 3:14-19 *(New Living Translation)*

The church in Laodicea had become indifferent towards God. They were unaffected by Him due to their satisfaction with their earthly elevation. They had become lukewarm, and the Lord had to tell them that they had nothing, were nothing, and would amount to nothing in the end if they carried on with their comfortable lifestyle.

He advised them to become passionate and enthusiastic, to do away with their indifference, to seek Him and what He has to offer them. This message, just as those of the other churches, was meant to address issues in the specific congregations.

★★★

Anyone who was watching or listening to all these different messages by the different preachers would be very confused and would not really address the specific issues in their own lives.

The Apostle of your church will have the doctrine that is good for you, and your proper development depends on you following it.

> *"That we henceforth be no more children, tossed to and fro, and carried about with every wind of doctrine, by the sleight of men, and cunning craftiness, whereby they lie in wait to deceive;"*
>
> *- Ephesians 4:14*

AVOIDING FALSE DOCTRINES

Just as there is counterfeit money because there is an original, there are counterfeit doctrines ready to lead unaware and unsuspecting Christians astray.

> *Now the Spirit speaketh expressly, that in the latter times some shall depart from the faith, giving heed to seducing spirits and doctrines of devils.*
>
> *- 1 Timothy 4:1*

There are two types of false doctrines to be aware of. These are **Doctrines of Devils** and **Pseudo Word**.

Some doctrines are openly erroneous and clearly false. These are easy to spot. The greater danger lies in the Pseudo Word. These are spouted by seducing spirits to lead the unsuspecting into sweet-sounding but unfounded doctrines.

These teachings sound good. Some are even scriptural, but the

Scriptures are being used out of context and thus generating a new wise and spiritual-sounding teaching which is scripturally unsound.

Every good pastor faces this temptation because they genuinely love and care for the people they are leading and are moved by their plights. Sympathy and desperation easily lead ministers to preach biblical messages which address the members' hopes, dreams, desires and needs when it is not what God has asked them to do.

> *"Take heed unto thyself and unto the doctrine; continue in them: for in doing this thou shalt both save thyself and them that hear thee."*
>
> *- 1 Timothy 4:16*

Every minister must protect themselves from this by doing what God has called them to do and preaching what God has called them to preach. Every Christian must protect themselves from being taken advantage of by deepening their personal relationship with God, by checking what they are taught against the Scriptures and by *remaining* where God has planted them.

CHURCH LEADERSHIP

"... of these men which have companied with us all the time that the Lord Jesus went in and out among us, beginning from the baptism of John, unto that same day that he was taken up from us, must one be ordained ..."

- Acts 1:21-22

Leaders in the church are appointed by inspiration of the Holy Spirit. These are people with qualities like faithfulness, wisdom, and the presence and power of the Holy Spirit. Giftings and charisma are secondary.

It is very dangerous to appoint a leader who has not been with you for a long time because they have not been tried and proven faithful. There is no guarantee that they have caught the God-given vision of the church or learnt the way things are done.

They may not even know, let alone fully believe in the doctrines of the apostle of the church. These things are seen and corrected over time. This is known as catching the spirit of the church or house.

A member should not expect to be appointed a leader when they have not been planted for any length of time and when they have not fully imbibed the spirit of the church they are in.

Being planted and deeply rooted in a place is a vital component of being a leader in the Church. This is why, after Judas died, one of the qualifications of the one who replaced him was someone who had been in their company right from the start.

Leaders are also expected to be spiritual and full of the Holy Spirit. When the apostles chose people to do anything in church, they did not look for gifts, talents, or abilities. They looked for those who were full of the Holy Spirit and wisdom (the practical application of the Word of God). (See Acts 6:5-6.)

When Paul wrote to Timothy and Titus, he gave each a list of traits to look out for when appointing people to leadership positions in the Church. He was very specific about these characteristics because they are very important when it comes to being a leader.

Many are unaware of this, so they often use gifts, talents, achievements, status, charisma, and even good looks to judge who should lead or who to follow.

The Church of God cannot be run as a democracy. Because someone is a successful orator or businessman, it does not mean they will make a good president. I have met charismatic orators in church who have spent over an hour impressing me with beautiful speeches without ever answering the Bible study question that brought me to them in the first place.

People who do not understand this principle of appointment often criticise church leaders. This is because the one in a leadership role, such as the worship leader, prayer leader, and even the pastor, may not necessarily measure up to their idea of who should be chosen to lead.

It is true that it is not always the one with the best voice or talent that makes the best worship leader. Over my nine years of experience working with minstrels and worship leaders, I have seen that the best of them—the ones who have truly ministered the presence of God—tend not to have any spectacular gifts or talents. Most of them could not even sing well.

Having said all this, I will not neglect that some leaders may not be the best kind of people to take up that role. I agree that some people are wrong in their leadership roles, but remember, Judas was appointed by Jesus himself, and he was put in that position for a reason. Even those we see as bad leaders have been put there for a reason in God's divine plan.

It is important to understand that the Church is under the authority of Christ, and in positions of authority those within it, although appointed by men, have actually been placed there by God.

I strongly believe God is capable of displacing and replacing people. I also strongly believe He does not need anyone's permission or help to do so. If God does not like something, He will change it. I have seen it happen many times before.

> "Let every soul be subject unto the higher powers. For there is no power but of God: the powers that be are ordained of God. Whosoever therefore resisteth the power, resisteth the ordinance of God: and they that resist shall receive to themselves damnation."
>
> - Romans 13:1-2

THE ROLE OF CHURCH LEADERS

> "Obey them that have the rule over you, and submit yourselves: for they watch for your souls, as they that must give account, that they may do it with joy, and not with grief: for that is unprofitable for you."
>
> - Hebrews 13:17

Leaders are appointed over different sections of the Church and the congregation to provide adequate care for the people of God.

In chapter six of the Acts of the Apostles, a crisis arose in the early Church. People were not being cared for as they should have been. To resolve this problem, leaders were appointed.

Notice that the positions Stephen and the others occupied were not vacant and waiting for them, these positions were created to solve a new problem. The whole purpose of leadership is to solve the problems of the people, to care for them and watch over their souls.

In the same way the apostles appointed people to provide adequate care for the widows in the Church, so also Moses appointed the seventy elders to provide adequate care for the children of Israel.

Although Moses was the one who called and chose the seventy elders, it was an instruction from God Himself. God told Moses to appoint leaders to help him bear the burden of the people so that they would receive adequate care. (See Numbers 11:10-17.)

Church leaders are appointed to help the head leader care for the congregation. These leaders have an expectation from God to give an account of the people under them, to watch over the souls of the people they have been given to take care of. Therefore, it is important for them to get to know and help those people.

The problem they encounter is that people are often closed and suspicious of others. They find it bothersome when some church leaders look out for them.

Understanding that the role of a spiritual leader in your life is to watch over your soul and to give account to God changes the way people relate with Church Leadership.

HOW TO RELATE WITH CHURCH LEADERSHIP

1. Relate well by being obedient and submissive

"Obey them that have the rule over you, and submit yourselves: for they watch for your souls, as they that must give account, that they may do it with joy, and not with grief: for that is unprofitable for you."

- Hebrews 13:17

2. Relate well by honouring them

"Let the elders that rule well be counted worthy of double honour, especially they who labour in the word and doctrine."

- 1 Timothy 5:17

3. Relate well by not accusing them

"Against an elder receive not an accusation, but before two or three witnesses."

- 1 Timothy 5:19

4. Relate well by not rebuking them

"Rebuke not an elder, but entreat him as a father; and the younger men as brethren;"

- 1 Timothy 5:1

5. Relate well by praying for them

"Brethren, pray for us."

- 1 Thessalonians 5:25

SEVEN REASONS WHY EVERY CHRISTIAN SHOULD GO TO CHURCH

1. It is a biblical instruction to not forsake the gatherings of the brethren

"And let us consider one another to provoke unto love and to good works: not forsaking the assembling of ourselves together, as the manner of some is; but exhorting one another: and so much the more, as ye see the day approaching."

- Hebrews 10:24-25

2. It is a sign that you have the Holy Spirit in you

"These be they who separate themselves, sensual, having not the Spirit."

- Jude 1:19

3. Jesus is adding those he is saving to the Church

"...praising God, and having favour with all the people. And the Lord added to the church daily such as should be saved."

- Acts 2:47

4. To receive regular and consistent pastoral care

"Feed the flock of God which is among you, taking the oversight thereof, not by constraint, but willingly; not for filthy lucre, but of a ready mind;"

- 1 Peter 5:2

5. To fulfil that commandment of Christ

"This is my commandment, that ye love one another, as I have loved you."

- John 15:12

7. To fulfil your biblical calling of service to others

"For, brethren, ye have been called unto liberty; only use not liberty for an occasion to the flesh, but by love serve one another."

- Galatians 5:13

PART TWO:
REASONS CHRISTIANS GIVE FOR NOT GOING TO CHURCH

CHURCH IS BORING

"On the first day of the week we came together to break bread. Paul spoke to the people and, because he intended to leave the next day, kept on talking until midnight. There were many lamps in the upstairs room where we were meeting. Seated in a window was a young man named Eutychus, who was sinking into a deep sleep as Paul talked on and on. When he was sound asleep, he fell to the ground from the third story and was picked up dead. Paul went down, threw himself on the young man and put his arms around him. "Don't be alarmed," he said. "He's alive!" Then he went upstairs again and broke bread and ate. After talking until daylight, he left. The people took the young man home alive and were greatly comforted."

- Acts 20:7-12 (New International Version)

For whatever reason, it is common to find people falling asleep in church. Some fall asleep because they are tired after working a night shift or having a difficult week. People fall asleep because they are generally disinterested in the message and are only at church to fulfil all righteousness, and some, sadly, fall asleep because the service is boring.

Falling asleep in church is not a new thing and, we can see that when Paul preached in the early Church, someone slept so deeply that he fell out of the third-floor window. But because someone has fallen asleep in church, it does not automatically mean that church is boring.

I remember once, back in high school, I attended a mass where the priest was giving a very sound homily. We had had a busy day at school, it was very hot, and everyone in the chapel felt really drowsy. But we did what we could to stay awake and attentive.

After a long battle, my mind began to wander, and I honestly think I had just stepped over the threshold into the territory of dozing.

Suddenly, I heard a loud slap. My eyes shot open, mind snapped into focus, ready to run or prove that I was not asleep, if need be. After a moment—and confirming that I had not been caught—I noticed disruption at the front of the chapel.

A girl sitting at the edge of the pew had fallen asleep, toppled over the armrest, and fallen right into the central aisle in the middle of mass.

I will be honest, on several occasions in my youth, I have nodded off so far that I have banged my head on the pew in front of me.

People falling asleep does not mean church is boring. It does not subtract from the power of God. Do not be discouraged or put off when people fall asleep in church. Even Paul, whose writings make up a major part of the Bible, had someone fall asleep and die as he preached.

A lot of fun and interesting things happen at church, and once I took an interest in spiritual things, even exhausted and fatigued from the activities of the day, I have found I am rarely bored or uninterested in the things going on in church.

> *"Thou wilt shew me the path of life: in thy presence is fulness of joy;*
> *At thy right hand there are pleasures for evermore."*
>
> *- Psalm 16:11*

Developing an interest in the things and people of God will make church services less boring.

Christianity is about your personal relationship with Christ and your spiritual growth in him. The actions of others should not deter you from that. Remember, you will be held accountable for YOUR actions.

CHRISTIANS DON'T GET ALONG

"I beseech Euodias, and beseech Syntyche, that they be of the same mind in the Lord. And I intreat thee also, true yokefellow, help those women which laboured with me in the gospel, with Clement also, and with other my fellowlabourers, whose names are in the book of life."

- Philippians 4:2-3

The Church consists of people from different backgrounds, with different thoughts, ideas and ways of doing things. This makes it normal, and even expected, that people will not always get along.

Some give this as an excuse for not joining a church. They say, "I don't want to see so and so," or "These church people are annoying."

It is unfair to write-off a whole group of people for the actions of one or two individuals. We have all done wrong, and in many ways, we offend others. But God forgives us of our unrighteousness, and we expect people to forgive us when we offend them.

In the verse above, we see Paul begging for reconciliation between two women in the early Church who seemed not to be getting along.

"Your love for one another will prove to the world that you are my disciples."

- John 13:35 (New Living Translation)

The Church is full of imperfect people serving a perfect God. We all, in our own ways, offend and will be offended by many. Let us be merciful and try to get along for Christ's sake, if nothing else.

Christianity is about your personal relationship with Christ and your spiritual growth in him. The actions of others should not deter you from that. Remember, you will be held accountable for YOUR actions.

I FEEL I DON'T BELONG

"For it hath been declared unto me of you, my brethren, by them which are of the house of Chloe, that there are contentions among you. Now this I say, that every one of you saith, I am of Paul; and I of Apollos; and I of Cephas; and I of Christ."

- 1 Corinthians 1:11-12

Fact: Cliques exist in churches.

Deny it as many may, it is true that people gravitate to those they have things in common with, be it tribe, colour, interests, or professions, to name a few.

Though many may not segregate themselves in such natural and obvious ways, a lot end up doing so by ministries, interests, and sometimes even leadership preferences.

In the earlier scripture, members of the early Church divided themselves based on who pastored them. This still happens today. I have been to conferences where people from branches of the same Church in the Southern cities did not fraternize with those from the Northern cities simply because they were under a different General Overseer.

It is sad but true. Even when we do not segregate ourselves for natural reasons, our human nature leads us to spot and magnify the differences between ourselves and other people. This is something we must be aware of and fight against as Christians.

The reality is that Christians are human too, and as with any other group of humans, people gravitate to those they are comfortable with, unintentionally leaving others out.

It is a real issue, an issue Paul constantly confronted in the early Church. But Paul never confirmed it as a good enough excuse to stay away from the gathering of believers.

Many guilty of this cliquing are genuinely ignorant of your feelings. They honestly may have no clue that you feel left out or like you do not belong. Do not cut yourself off from where God has put you because of how some unknowingly make you feel.

For a long time after I joined my church, I felt left out, unwanted, and like I did not belong. To date (as I write this) some of the closest friends I have now are those I made in church, and I would not trade them for anything. I'm glad I stayed despite the way I felt.

Christianity is about your personal relationship with Christ and your spiritual growth in him. The actions of others should not deter you from that. Remember, you will be held accountable for YOUR actions.

PEOPLE IN CHURCH ARE PROUD

"Now some are puffed up, as though I would not come to you. But I will come to you shortly, if the Lord will, and will know, not the speech of them which are puffed up, but the power."

- 1 Corinthians 4:18

Pride is the invisible enemy that creeps up on well-meaning, unsuspecting believers.

Sometimes, because of who they have become, what they have gained or accomplished, and sometimes, for no reason at all, people see themselves as greater, higher, or better than they actually are. They relate with others as such, and lean on their own strength, forgetting that it is the grace of God that has enabled them to do, have and be.

This is common with human beings everywhere, and since human beings are in the Church, such people or behaviours will be present.

It is imperative that you notice such traits in yourself in order to run your Christian race well.

There are a number of ways to detect pride in oneself, and there are extensive teachings on this topic. One easy way to identify pride in yourself is how often you feel the need to talk about yourself (in both positive and negative ways).

It is illogical and almost impossible to advise one not to think or talk about oneself. Everyone stands at the centre of the axis their individual world revolves around. But take care when your thoughts and conversations *need* to centre around you. It is a clear sign that you have become your focus. And anything you focus on becomes magnified, removing your focus from God. That includes yourself.

Christianity is about your personal relationship with Christ and your spiritual growth in him. The actions of others should not deter you from that. Remember, you will be held accountable for YOUR actions.

PEOPLE IN CHURCH ARE NOSY SNITCHES WHO REPORT EVERYTHING TO THE PASTOR

"For I rejoiced greatly, when the brethren came and testified of the truth that is in thee, even as thou walkest in the truth."

- 3 John 1:3

A church is a spiritual organization run by Spirt-filled, Spirit-led *people*. Naturally, there will always be an appraisal of performance. There is also the need for accountability, and the head leader is the person who is held accountable for everything that goes on in that church.

This is one reason why it is important for the pastors or leadership of the church to know what is going on.

Another reason for things to be reported is because the leadership is interested in the wellbeing and spiritual development of its members. They need to be aware of where each person is and what they need in their walk with God if they are to provide the necessary care and accountability needed.

> *"For it hath been declared unto me of you, my brethren, by them which are of the house of Chloe, that there are contentions among you. Now this I say, that every one of you saith, I am of Paul; and I of Apollos; and I of Cephas; and I of Christ."*
>
> *- 1 Corinthians 1:11-12*

When something goes wrong and it is reported, it is not because people are snitches or gossips. Granted, sometimes it is. Sometimes people try to garner favour by gossiping because people will inevitably be people. But whatever they say does not—and should never—affect a leader's perception of the believers under their care.

When leaders are made aware of a situation, whatever the source, it is to enlighten them on where and how to direct their guidance. The leader will identify a gossip who needs guidance.

The Word is not for encouragement alone, it is also for reproof and correction, to make sure the believer is thoroughly furnished unto all good works.

> *"All scripture is given by inspiration of God, and is profitable for doctrine, for reproof, for correction, for instruction in righteousness: that the man of God may be perfect, thoroughly furnished unto all good works."*
>
> *- 2 Timothy 3:16-17*

Christianity is about your personal relationship with Christ and your spiritual growth in him. The actions of others should not deter you from that. Remember, you will be held accountable for YOUR actions.

THERE ARE SO MANY THINGS WRONG WITH THE CHURCH

> *"... that he might sanctify and cleanse it with the washing of water by the word, that he might present it to himself a glorious church, not having spot, or wrinkle, or any such thing; but that it should be holy and without blemish."*
>
> *- Ephesians 5:26-27*

The history of the Church is one of bloodshed and politics alongside spirituality and the moving of God. This makes people sometimes sceptical of the Church as a whole. It is true the Church may have made many mistakes along the way, but Jesus is working on it to cleanse it and change all of that.

> *"Wherefore, if I come, I will remember his deeds which he doeth, prating against us with malicious words: and not content therewith, neither doth he himself receive the brethren, and forbiddeth them that would, and casteth them out of the church."*
>
> *- 3 John 1:10*

It is true that, while we wait and are growing, there are other mistakes that will be made and things that will be done wrong in genuinely good conscience as well as malice.

Christians are held to a different standard of judgement from others. Both within and without, some stand idly by, watching and critically passing judgement, or waiting for something to go wrong just so they can talk about it.

They criticize the leadership, the people, the singing and the dancing, the way people dress, the preaching, the sound, the worship, the lighting, the temperature, the seats, and the size of the hall. They will criticize anything to do with the Church. They will even critically interview Jesus and bombard him with questions on morally and politically grey areas in the scripture if he physically steps into the church.

It is easier to find fault with something one is not involved with. When one stands aloof and uninvolved in building the Church, it becomes very easy to criticize whatever they think is going wrong.

It is easier to speak maliciously about something one is not involved or invested in. No one will admit that the football team they support is the worst, no matter how bad the team is. It is their team. Blues were, are, and will forever be the best. And it is simply not up for discussion with me.

So also, with the Church, when one supports the house of God, one finds ways to the fix or forgive its faults.

I am not stupid. The Church is not perfect. The congregation are not perfect. The Bible says it is *being made* perfect. It is an imperfect community, run and loved by a perfect God who is very capable of changing anything that He does not want.

Perhaps the problem you have noticed is the problem God wants you to fix, or the problem God is using to fix something in you. If others have not noticed it is a problem, perhaps God has revealed it to you alone.

And if it is truly a problem, why not pray about it instead of criticizing it and not allowing it to uproot you from the body of Christ.

Christianity is about your personal relationship with Christ and your spiritual growth in him. The actions of others should not deter you from that. Remember, you will be held accountable for YOUR actions.

PEOPLE IDOLISE PREACHERS

Idolizing people is not new or strange. Across eras, cultures, and religions, people of significance have been idolised. We have myths and legends which have grown around individuals that have been idolized. We have statues erected in honour of great achievers. Universities, colleges, and entire schools of thought have been dedicated to the study and teachings of influential people.

Preachers are influential people. It is unsurprising for some to idolize them. But there is a difference between being enamoured of a person, being deeply grateful to them, loving and honouring them, and idolizing them.

Understand this, a preacher is only made significant by the message they preach. The truth is: the most significant thing about a prophet is the message from God that they convey.

When people do not listen to or obey the message, but exalt and honour the prophet, they idolize the prophet, making him no greater than a mute golden calf who has been declared as holy, and a chosen vessel of God.

The prophet cannot be faulted for the actions of the people.

However, when it is brought to their awareness that the people honour them more than the message of God that they are delivering, like in the case of Paul and Barnabas, the responsibility falls on the prophet or preacher to stop the people from doing so.

In Acts 14:11-15, Paul and Barnabas preached to some people to turn to God, but the people were more focused on exalting them for the miracle they had done than listening to the message they preached. If they had listened to Paul's message to turn to the one true God, they would not have decided that Paul and Barnabas were gods come down to them, something completely contrary to the message preached.

THE PROPHET OF GOD SHOULD BE HONOURED

"But Jesus, said unto them, a prophet is not without honour, but in his own country, and among his own kin, and in his own house."

- Mark 6:4

A prophet is to be honoured. It would bring a terrible curse upon the Church to dishonour their fathers and leaders. The Bible contains instructions to honour teachers, prophets, leaders, and parents for who they are. They are who they are because of their closeness to God.

They have given their lives to building the kingdom of God and have sacrificed very much for the church they are being honoured in to even exist. They deserve to be honoured and remembered.

Honour is not idolatry. It is an important spiritual practice. You will not exist without your parents and that is why parents must be honoured. The church you are in and your relationship with God (the most important relationship in your life) would probably not exist without your spiritual leader. For that alone, they deserve to be honoured.

Christianity is about your personal relationship with Christ and your spiritual growth in him. The actions of others should not deter you from that. Remember, you will be held accountable for YOUR actions.

CHRISTIANS ARE HYPOCRITES

A hypocrite is someone who pretends to be something that they are not. Hypocrisy is rooted in lies and dishonesty.

Ananias and Sapphira were a couple in the early Church who saw early believers sell their lands and give the money to the Church. The early believers were very dedicated and very spiritual. So, Ananias and his wife wanted to look the same way. The only problem was, they weren't.

The couple sold their land and brought the money to the apostles. But instead of just being honest about how much they were giving, they lied that they had given all they had made from the sale.

The couple got struck dead for their lie. (See Acts 5:1-5.)

It is true that many believers are more concerned about the outward show of spirituality than the inner workings of the spirit. Some Christians lie and pretend, living their lives as hypocrites, and nothing seems to happen to them.

Understand that their judgement is left to God and no one else. Notice that Peter told Ananias that he had lied to the Holy Ghost and not to himself (Peter). Judgement is for God and no one else.

Read on in the story and you will find that the hypocrisy of Ananias and Sapphira did not deter people from being added to the Church.

> *"... and believers were more added to the Lord, multitudes both of men and women..."*
>
> - Acts 5:14

Christianity is about your personal relationship with Christ and your spiritual growth in him. The actions of others should not deter you from that. Remember, you will be held accountable for YOUR actions.

GOD IS EVERYWHERE AND JESUS IS IN MY HEART

"For where two or three are gathered together in my name, there am I in the midst of them."

- Matthew 18:20

A common reason Christians give for not attending Church gatherings is that God is omnipresent, and they do not need to be in one specific place for Him to speak to them.

The devil is a master strategist and one of his greatest strategies is isolation. In wildlife, predators look out for or try to isolate their prey before over-powering it. This is a tactic the devil employs when dealing with Christians: to isolate and then attack while they can be overpowered easily.

Do not fall for his trap.

Jesus promises to be where his people gather. It is true that we can worship God at home and create an environment where the Spirit of God flows, but Jesus is building his Church and part of that building project requires the people to gather.

One is not an assembly.

God calls individuals and puts them in churches. Even when one has no need for what the gathering has to offer, one is required to offer something to others also.

Yes, God is everywhere and the Holy Ghost lives in our hearts, we believe Jesus is the son of God who died to take away our sins. This is the very beginning of your Christianity. Now, our spirits need to grow, and that requires being taught.

It is true Jesus is in every believer's heart, but a clear sign of the presence of Jesus is that people gather in his name. When you truly have Jesus and love God, you will want to be with His people in spite of and despite their issues and faults.

Christianity is about your personal relationship with Christ and your spiritual growth in him. The actions of others should not deter you from that. Remember, you will be held accountable for YOUR actions.

OTHER EXCUSES

SINFULNESS

"Everyone who does evil hates the light, and will not come into the light for fear that their deeds will be exposed."

- John 3:20 (New International Version)

Believers fall into sin. The guilt of it can make one feel unworthy or judged, and result in them staying away from other believers. The natural effect of sin is hiding. In the garden of Eden, when man sinned against God, they became aware of their nakedness and their natural reaction was to hide from His presence. We do the same when we become aware of our sinful nature. This results in us staying away from church.

The Church is not to be a place of judgement and condemnation. In fact, it can be likened to a hospital, full of sick people waiting to receive care. To receive the right care, openness is key.

Imagine going to see your doctor because you are suffering from severe stomach pain, but when your doctor asks where the pain is, what kind of pain it is, if you are eating well, sexually active, allergic to anything or have done any form of strenuous abdominal exercises of late, you decide the doctor is being nosy, or you prefer not to be asked such personal questions.

Without being open and honest with the doctor, one cannot get the help they need.

Granted, a spiritual leader may not need to ask those specific questions, but they do need to ask those pertaining to one's life and godliness. And without being open with one's spiritual leader, one cannot get the help one needs.

SENSUALITY

"These be they who separate themselves, sensual, having not the Spirit."

- Jude 1:19

To be sensual simply means to be ruled by one's senses. Many do not attend services because they just do not feel like it on that day.

Some say things like, "I don't feel like Church today," or, "I'm tired and I feel like I need my rest." These are the type who miss service because of 19 drops of rain.

One ruled by their senses will be unstable in their commitment to the assembly since their actions and decisions depend mainly on how they feel at any given point in time.

OTHERS WHO HAVE LEFT

"For Demas hath forsaken me, having loved this present world, and is departed unto Thessalonica; Crescens to Galatia, Titus unto Dalmatia.

- 2 Timothy 4:10

It is not always the case that when people leave a church, there was something wrong with it. People leave for different reasons.

Demas, Crescens, and Titus while on the missionary journeys, left because the work of God had to be done in different places, not due to any existing issues. They were transferred or sent for the benefit of the Church as a whole.

Imagine quitting your job because someone else in your office got sacked, resigned or got transferred. Or moving to a new house because your neighbour no longer likes the neighbourhood or because they got a better job in another state.

Your actions and commitment to the church God has placed you in should not be based on someone else's, but on a conviction that it is where God wants you to be.

ITCHING EARS

"For the time will come when they will not endure sound doctrine; but after their own lusts shall they heap to themselves teachers, having itching ears; And they shall turn away their ears from the

> truth, and shall be turned unto fables."
>
> - 2 Timothy 4:3-4

Some leave churches because the Word being preached is not what they want to hear. They choose to believe what they like and refuse to listen to the truth because it makes them feel uncomfortable or goes against their desires (lusts).

That some will refuse sound doctrine is true in this age of liberality and freedom.

THE LOVE OF THE WORLD

> "For Demas hath forsaken me, having loved this present world, and is departed unto Thessalonica;"
>
> - 2 Timothy 4:10

God loves everyone in the world, and He expects us to do the same. However, He holds no love for the things of this world. This is what many Christians get wrong.

The god of this world is running it straight to hell, along with anyone who chooses to follow it. If a red creature with horns and a pitchfork appeared in the city square and said, "Follow me to hell," it is unlikely anyone would.

The devil may not be a little pitchfork-wielding, red demon, but the concept remains true. The god of this world entices with the things one desires and those who chase these things are unwittingly following him.

The pleasures of this world are a carrot, dangled on a stick being held by the devil. Chasing after it will lead away from the Church of God.

MORE TYPES OF PEOPLE YOU WILL FIND IN THE CHURCH

The Church is full of all types of people, with different abilities, different motivations, different problems, from their very different lives.

The Church is full of imperfect people. Some do their best to know and serve God, some are happy to get along with being lukewarm. Some are the tares that the enemy sows in the Lord's field to destroy the harvest.

Being aware of this is important, and not letting another's walk determine or affect one's own is key. (See Romans 12:3-8.)

A few types of people one will find in the Church include:

THE SONS AND DAUGHTERS

"To Timothy, my dearly beloved son: Grace, mercy, and peace, from God the Father and Christ Jesus our Lord."

- 2 Timothy 1:2

Relationships develop, and a relationship between a spiritual leader and their member often develops into a filial one. It is normal for one who has been spiritually birthed, raised and trained to regard their mentor or leader as a parent figure, or for one who has done the birthing and raising to regard their mentee as they would their own child.

THE TEACHERS

"And God hath set some in the church, first apostles, secondarily prophets, thirdly teachers, after that miracles, then gifts of healings, helps, governments, diversities of tongues."

- 1 Corinthians 12:28

There is a knowledge and understanding of God which every Christian must receive. God places teachers among His people to impart this knowledge. These teachers have a depth of understanding and revelation of the scripture, and possess a gift to break it down in such a way that others understand it.

THE PROPHETS

"And God hath set some in the church, first apostles, secondarily prophets, thirdly teachers, after that miracles, then gifts of healings, helps, governments, diversities of tongues."

- 1 Corinthians 12:28

A prophet is an agent of change. A prophet speaks the mind of God. A prophet is one who the Lord regards as His friend, a friend He can reveal secrets to, and a messenger He can trust to deliver those secrets to those He intended them for. A prophet speaks, and it comes to pass because they speak the Word of God.

THE APOSTLES

"And God hath set some in the church, first apostles, secondarily prophets, thirdly teachers, after that miracles, then gifts of healings, helps, governments, diversities of tongues."

- 1 Corinthians 12:28

An apostle in the Church today is someone who builds, starts or founds churches. Some have the gift of *breaking ground*, that is, going to different places to start and establish branches.

THE FAITHFUL BRETHREN

"To the saints and faithful brethren in Christ which are at Colosse: Grace be unto you, and peace, from God our Father and the Lord Jesus Christ."

- Colossians 1:2

Most people are loyal to whatever suits them, for as long as it does. It is a blessing to find someone who is faithful to God and to His Church even when it is difficult. Faithfulness is a rare and precious virtue.

The faithful are different from the regular saints and good-sounding members of the Church. Faithful people are special people.

THE WORKERS

"Aristarchus my fellow prisoner saluteth you, and Marcus, sister's son to Barnabas, (touching whom ye received commandments: if he come unto you, receive him;) and Jesus, which is called Justus, who are of the circumcision. These only are my fellowworkers unto the kingdom of God, which have been a comfort unto me. Epaphras, who is one of you, a servant of Christ, saluteth you, always labouring fervently for you in prayers, that ye may stand perfect and complete in all the will of God."

- Colossians 4:10-12

Most think building and running a Church is easy. The truth is God's work is hard and it takes people with determination and diligence to accomplish it. It requires time, money, energy, and labour. The lazy cannot work for God.

THE FALSE PROPHETS AND TEACHERS

"But there were false prophets also among the people, even as there shall be false teachers among you, who privily shall bring in damnable heresies, even denying the Lord that bought them, and bring upon themselves swift destruction."

- 2 Peter 2:1

A counterfeit can only exist when there is a real thing to copy. Prophets and teachers are gifts from God, they are valuable to the body of Christ. Individuals with gifts of prophecy and teaching who are not being led by the Spirit of God will give false teachings and counterfeit words from God.

The words themselves may be of God, but if it is not sent from God, but taken out of context and shared at the whim of a person, it is a false word.

THE GOOD LEADERS

"Remember your leaders who taught you the word of God. Think of all the good that has come from their lives, and follow the example of their faith."

- Hebrews 13:7 (New Living Translation)

There are good and bad leaders. A good leader has a vision to get people to a particular destination, a spiritual vision for their followers to reach a particular place in their walk with God. A good leader enables by teaching the skills necessary to survive without them.

One important trait in a good leader is the ability to lead by example.

A leader is someone in front, someone who goes before. They pave a safe path ahead, they are at the frontline during any attack, and solve any problems that arise, all so their followers walk safely. How useful is a guide who is as lost and clueless as one is?

Good leaders do not instruct from the comfort of an armchair, they are practical, hands-on examples of what to do, and what one can become. They encourage as they guide.

A WORD OF CAUTION

"He that is not with me is against me; and he that gathereth not with me scattereth abroad."

- Matthew 12:30

The Church is the body of Christ, the gathering of believers in the name of Jesus. It is an imperfect group of people brought together by their belief in and love for a perfect God. One will always find faults in anything if one looks hard enough.

Jesus gave his life for his Church. He came to seek and save, to gather his people. This includes you. To exempt oneself from the gathering is to stand in opposition to what Jesus is doing.

Life and circumstances may not permit one to attend on a regular basis, and it would be unreasonable to ask of one to do more than they physically can. But when one's separation is due to a separation of the heart, a dangerous line is being towed.

Christians go to Church because they are the different parts of one body, different members of the great family of God, and because it is in the Church that they are purified and made holy by the Word of God and their communion with one another.

"And they entered into a covenant to seek the LORD God of their fathers with all their heart and with all their soul;"

-2 Chronicles 15:12

MY PRAYER FOR YOU

My prayer and heart's cry for you is that you come to know and experience the Lord personally and intimately, and that this knowledge of Him transforms you from the inside, out.

ACKNOWLEDGEMENTS

After many years of seeking to know God personally, I am grateful that He has chosen me as a vessel to carry this message to the world, and most especially, to His beloved children.

Much appreciation goes to all the wonderful individuals who have played a part in my journey to completing this work, whose names if I were to list, would likely fill the pages of the book twice over.

I am truly humbled and grateful to you all.

To my mother, Priye: Thank you for your love and your sacrifice, for your faith and your prayers, for being my lighthouse during the storms, and my rock when I needed a solid foundation. There are no words to express how great you are, and how much your silent strength has inspired me to become the woman that I am today. I owe it all to you.

My Pastor and spiritual father, Reverend Dr. Stephen K. Poku, who took the time to patiently teach me how to practically live out the lessons and principles in this book: thank you for your unrelenting faith and trust in me.

Also, to my other mothers—Tonye, Amonia, and Dawn—who

have been with me all these years, and supported me through many difficult times in life, thank you for being the great blessing that you are.

Uncle Odein, thank you for believing and investing in me, for being there to catch me whenever I fell, for giving me wings to fly, and proving to me that I've always had a father, even at times when I felt I had none.

Reverend Boanerge Yamoah, thank you for seeing God's hand on my life, and then pushing me forward even when I was unwilling to go.

Ellen Netty, who has led me by the hand like she would her own daughter—and also taken me out to dinner in London on a yearly standing reservation since the first day we met.

Edna Tsenuokpor, for being the light that guided me through some of the darkest tunnels I walked through. It's always been a great pleasure serving in your ministry.

Samira Otung, thank you for taking the time to read *Show Me Your Glory* and offer words of wisdom and encouragement. Thank you for being a sister and friend.

Bishop Eddy Addy, whose teachings inspired me to seek and know God for myself.

And also, Georgette Yeboah, thank you for always having my back with those instrumentalists. You have always been a great friend and a pleasure to work with.

Reverend Tsidi, minister of joy. Words cannot express how grateful I am to know you.

Daniel Oware-Amankwaah, all those ministration lessons and trips to Manchester were not in vain. I owe you so much, and I will never forget that.

Claire Glover, thank you for all your hard work and diligence in bringing the audiobook to life with your wonderful narration.

My editors and friends, Neliya, Dera and Doxie, I appreciate all your prayers and support and tireless effort.

My wonderful patrons who believe in and faithfully support my writing: Dr. T. Wokoma, C. Omeje, T. Okoye, S. Obomanu.

Aunty Sandy, simply because we still want this to remain as one book, I will just mention your name and say thank you.

Diana Pillay, thank you for taking my hand and leading me. For teaching me and being there for as long as you were here.

And again, to my mother who is always right, I love you mucho.

BIBLIOGRAPHY

- Avanzini, J. (1992) *It's not working brother John*. Abel Press
- Bounds, E. M. (2004) *The Complete Works of E. M. Bounds on prayer: Experience the Wonders of God Through Prayer*. Baker Books
- Bounds, E. M. (2013) *Complete Works of E. M. Bounds*. Simon and Schuster
- Hagin, K. E. (1975) *Why Tongues*. Kenneth Hagin Ministries
- Hagin, K. E. (1976) *Growing up spiritually*. Faith Library Publications
- Hagin, K. E. (1980) *How to turn your faith loose*. Faith Library Publications
- Hagin, K. E. (1980) *Prayer that gets results*. Faith Library Publications
- Hagin, K. E. (1983) *Exceedingly growing faith*. Faith Library Publications
- Hagin, K. E. (1983) *Prayer secrets*, 2nd Ed. Faith Library Publication
- Hagin, K. E. (1984) *I believe in visions*. Faith Library Publications

- Hagin, K. E. (1984) *Understanding the anointing*. Faith Library Publications
- Hagin, K. E. (1987) *The Holy Spirit and His gifts*, 2nd Ed. Kenneth Hagin Ministries
- Hagin, K. E. (1991) *The art of prayer*, 4th Revised Ed. Faith Library Publication
- Hagin, K. E. (1991) *The interceding Christian*. Faith Library Publications
- Hagin, K. E. (1995) *The real faith*. Faith Library Publications
- Hagin, K. E. (2010) *Seven vital Keys to believing in the Holy Spirit*. Faith Library Publications
- Hagin, K. E. (2013) *what to do when faith seems weak & victory lost*. Faith Library Publications
- Hagin K. E. *The Spirit Within and the Spirit Upon*. Tulsa, Oklahoma: Kenneth Hagin Ministries, Inc., 2003.
- Heward-Mills D. *My Father, My Father*. Parchment House, 2004.
- Heward-Mills, D. (2004) *Quiet time*. Parchment House publications.
- Heward-Mills, D. (2007) *100% answered prayer*. Parchment house publications
- Heward-Mills, D. (2011) *Fathers and Loyalty*, 1st Edition; Parchment house publications

- Heward-Mills, D. (2013) *The sweet influences of the anointing*.
- Heward-Mills, D. (2014) *How to be born again and avoid hell*. Parchment house
- Heward-Mills, D. (2018) *Losing, suffering, sacrificing and dying*. Parchment house publications
- Heward-Mills, D. (2018) *Read your bible, pray everyday*. Parchment house publications
- Heward-Mills, D. (2019) *Faith Secrets*. Parchment House publications
- Heward-Mills, D. (2019) *Flow in the anointing*. Parchment house publications
- Heward-Mills, D. (2019) *Those who honour you*. Parchment House publications
- Hinn, B. (1990) *Good morning Holy Spirit*. Thomas Nelson.
- Hinn, B. (1997) *The anointing*, 2nd Ed. Thomas Nelson.
- Hinn, B. (2005) *Going deeper with the Holy Spirit*. Clarion Call Marketing.
- Johnson B. Hosting *The Presence*. Shippensburg, PA: Destiny Image Publishers, Inc., 2012.
- Johnson, B. & Vallotton, K. (2013). *The Supernatural Ways of Royalty*. Destiny Image
- Johnson, B. (2013). *When Heaven Invades Earth: A Practical Guide to a Life of Miracles*. Destiny Image

- Liardon, R. (2001) *God's Generals: V2.* Whitaker House
- Liardon, R. (2001) *God's Generals: Why They Succeeded and Why Some Failed.* Whitaker House
- Liardon, R. (2008) *God's Generals: The Revivalists.* Whitaker House
- Liardon, R. (2011) *God's Generals Healing Evangelists.* Whitaker House
- Liardon, R. (2014) *God's Generals: The Missionaries.* Whitaker House
- Liardon, R. (2016) *God's Generals: The Martyrs.* Whitaker House
- Maldonado G. *The Glory Of God.* New Kensington, PA: Whitaker House, 2012.
- Murray A. *Andrew Murray on the Holy Spirit.* New Kensington, PA: Whitaker House, 1998.
- Prince, D. (1993) *The Spirit-Filled Believers Handbook.* Creation House.
- Ravenhill L. *Revival Praying.* Bloomington, Minnesota: Bethany House Publishers, 2005.
- Silk, D. (2013) *Culture of Honor: Sustaining A Supernatural Environment.* Destiny Image
- Torrey, R. A. (1900) *How to pray.*
- Torrey, R. A. (1901) *The person and work of the Holy Spirit.*

- Torrey, R. A. (1985) *How to study the Bible*. United States, Whitaker House.
- Torrey, R. A. (2004) *Baptism of the Holy Spirit*. Bethany House Publishers
- Torrey, R. A. (2007) *Prayer and Faith*. United States, Whitaker House.
- Vallotton K. & Johnson B. *The supernatural ways of Royalty*. Shippensburg, PA: Destiny image Publishers, 2006.
- Wigglesworth, S. & Liardon, R. (2006) *Smith Wigglesworth on prayer, power and miracles*. Destiny Image Publishers
- Zschech D. *Extravagant Worship*. Bloomington, Minnesota: Bethany House Publishers, 2002.

CONNECT WITH XYVAH

Instagram: @xmokoye

Twitter: @xmokoye

Facebook: Xyvah M. Okoye

TikTok: @xmokoye

Subscribe to my blog: www.xyvahmokoye.com

Printed in Great Britain
by Amazon